Living LIKE A LAMB

AMONG 21ST CENTURY WOLVES

BALANCING GRACE AND TRUTH

PAUL ESTABROOKS

Paul Estabrooks

John 1:14

Library and Archives Canada Cataloguing in Publication
Title: **Living like a lamb among 21st century wolves : balancing grace and truth** / by Paul Estabrooks.
Other titles: Living like a lamb among twenty-first century wolves
Names: Estabrooks, Paul, author.
Identifiers: Canadiana 20230153844 | ISBN 9781988928784 (softcover)
Subjects: LCSH: Christian life. | LCSH: Christian ethics. | LCSH: Conduct of life.
Classification: LCC BV4501.3 .E88 2023 | DDC 248.4—dc23

CASTLE QUAY BOOKS

Contents

INTRODUCTION

Lambs are the cutest little animals, but totally vulnerable. We teach our children nursery rhymes about Mary taking one to school one day that the teacher expelled. The extra verses teach us that the lamb hung around outside the school waiting for Mary. The teacher assessed this was because Mary loved the lamb.

This book is about lambs. Jesus of Nazareth, the Lamb of God Himself, generated the imagery for the title. When He sent out seventy-two of His followers on a mission trip two-by-two (recorded in Luke 10), He said, "I am sending you out as lambs among wolves." All seventy-two came safely home but the imagery remains as a descriptive of those who create opposition. The very important subtitle of this volume comes from His closest disciple. John wrote a description of Jesus, the Word, in the prologue of his Gospel account of Jesus's life. He described Him as a person "full of grace and truth."

John went on to write about another John—John the Baptist, Jesus's cousin. When John the Baptist first introduced Jesus to the crowds to whom he was speaking, he said, "Look! The Lamb of God who takes away the sin of the world!" (John 1:29). The night before His crucifixion, Jesus celebrated the Passover with his twelve disciples. The primary food item was a Passover lamb commemorating the Exodus from Egypt.

Jesus took bread and wine at this celebration and instituted what we call the Eucharist or Holy Communion. After His resurrection, both the apostles Paul and Peter refer to Jesus as "our Passover Lamb." And the final book of the Bible pictures the resurrected Jesus in heaven with Father God. His name is "Lion of Judah," but He is pictured as a Lamb that looks like it had been slain. And the whole redemption story is completed with the wedding feast of the Lamb.

This is the very essence of the gospel that we who are Jesus followers believe and love to declare. Jesus became the substitutionary sacrifice for humankind mired in its sinfulness. Conquering the ultimate enemy, death, by His resurrection, Jesus provided forgiveness and a new and eternal life for those who follow Him.

So, it is not a stretch to picture those who decide to be followers of Jesus also as lambs. When Jesus challenged Peter about his love for Him, He said, "Feed my lambs." If we are to truly follow and serve Jesus as His lambs, we will also want to be those "full of grace and truth." To keep a balance of the two is the tightrope on which we walk.

Every year the Oxford Dictionary team chooses a new word-of-the-year. In 2016, our society's changing perspective on truth caused them to choose *post-truth* as the new single word that best summarized the change in our Western culture. They essentially defined this new word as truth now being based on feelings rather than facts; literally, relating to or denoting circumstances in which objective facts are less influential in shaping public opinion than appeals to emotion and personal belief. So now we talk about "your truth" and "my truth."

Many in this new post-truth culture are rejecting the old truth-based beliefs, and a tsunami of the reverberations is overwhelming our younger generation. Even what we older folk often refer to as just plain "common sense" is disappearing. And we followers of Jesus are facing more and more opposition to our biblically based principles of living. One of our notable theologians of the past generation, Francis Schaeffer, referred to these principles as "true truth."

My personal observations are that many of us reacting to this newly developed post-truth perspective, however, have become very strident and almost obnoxious in condemning it and counter-attacking—especially in social media. We are so focussed on re-establishing what we consider is objective truth that we have forgotten to balance truth with grace.

On the other hand, the years of pandemic we have recently experienced have prompted some of us to become passive and compliant. That is the essence of what I want to focus on in this writing, using story as well as biblical truth–based information.

In conflict situations, Christians have been historically divided into two opposing camps. One is called classic pacifism based on one perspective of Jesus's non-violence teaching. On the other side are those who firmly believe we are to make every effort and use every possible weapon to defend our freedoms and oppose tyranny. There is often a struggle with where one draws the line when it comes to violence or even self-defence.

Early church father Augustine began a process that centuries later Thomas Aquinas adapted called "just war," establishing principles or criteria for when a government should take violent action against an aggressor to ensure that a war is morally justifiable. It also is concerned with how to act within a war. You can find these criteria on the internet.

But what about conflict on a personal level? How far do you go with Jesus's instructions to "turn the other cheek"? Followers of Jesus—especially in countries of severe Christian persecution like Nigeria—have swung from classic pacifism, or aspects of non-violence on one hand, to physical retaliation in self-defence or violent aggression on the other.

Dr Glen Stassen has proposed a third way he calls "transforming initiatives." He believes Christians should direct their energies toward finding a set of criteria and a model for a "just peace" instead of just war. He bases his just peace theory on the new reality of our world, on recent biblical interpretation, and on the experiences of people who lived in the face of oppression and nuclear threat, and who—together with political scientists, Christian ethicists, and activists—fashion realistic steps toward peacemaking.[1]

Walter Wink also proposes a non-violent "third way" taught by Jesus. I discuss this third way with some applications learned from biblical teaching as well as from colleagues working with persecuted Christians around the world, people of faith who often feel like lambs for the slaughter (see Romans 8:36).

So, as we begin, let me paraphrase the old nursery rhyme this way:

Mary had a little lamb, He cleanses white as snow.

His life was full of grace and truth to mirror where you go.

PAUL ESTABROOKS

Let's start by evaluating that Bible story where the expression for this book's title is found.

1

WISE AS SNAKES AND HARMLESS AS DOVES

*Life at its best is a creative synthesis
of opposites in fruitful harmony.*

Martin Luther King Jr

A crowd began to assemble on a grassy hillside beside the sparkling Sea of Galilee. Those who were acquainted greeted one another with a loud "Shalom!" and a two-cheek holy kiss. Some were asking, "Do you know why the Master has called us here today?"

The well-known fisherman among them, Simon Peter, was telling one group, "This is where we, His chosen twelve, assembled to be briefed on our first mission trip."

Andrew was counting the crowd that now seemed to be complete. Seventy-two people! As he announced the number assembled, his colleague, John, spoke out to those standing around him. "This is a very symbolic assembly. There are seventy-two names in the Septuagint's first list of clans or nations in the Pentateuch. Perhaps we are somehow representing here all the nations of the world."

Simon the Zealot overheard the comment and was quick to point out that there were only seventy names listed in the early list of clans or nations in the Hebrew Torah.[2] As a patriot, he never did trust that Greek translation of the Torah, the Septuagint, even though it had been used throughout the Jewish diaspora for more than two hundred years and pointed many new readers to the one true God of Israel.

John broke in, "It really doesn't matter the actual number; it is indeed symbolic whichever list or number you use. Look, the Master is signalling us to come close and listen to his instructions."

Matthias didn't know others in the crowd very well, so he stuck close to John. This was the first time he had responded to a specific call to action from Jesus of Nazareth, even though he had known and followed Him from the day of His baptism. Jesus's call disrupted his daily routine, but it is said there is an adventurer hidden somewhere in the heart of everyone.

Jesus gestured for them to sit down and began, "You are each specially chosen for this very different kind of mission. Here's the big picture. I'm sending you out in pairs to all the towns and places that I later plan to visit. That includes Jewish towns and Gentile towns. You are representing me, and anyone rejecting you is rejecting me and my Father who sent me. You will go directly there with no stopping along the road. When you arrive, you will heal the sick and tell all the people that the Kingdom of God is now near you!

"Now, here are my four-step specific instructions. Note them well, as they are important to remember:

"One. You look like a sizeable crowd of my workers, but the harvest is great, and the workers are few. You will soon become very aware of this. So, your first step is to pray! Pray to the Lord who oversees the harvest. Ask Him to send more workers into His fields.

"Two. Go out remembering that I am sending you as lambs among wolves!"

Matthias shuddered. He had never suspected that working for Jesus of Nazareth could be dangerous. His family were shepherds and he had seen plenty of wolves take lambs from the flock. Unless their shepherd was close by, the lambs were defenseless and helpless before a strong, cunning, and deadly wolf. This analogy Jesus was using sounded more like exposure rather than protection.

Would he ever return to his wife and children? Yet he was impressed with Jesus's honesty. He trusted Jesus with his life, even though Jesus did not elaborate further on this "lambs among wolves" imagery.

Jesus was continuing: "Three. Travel light. Don't take any money, food, extra clothes, or sandals.

"Four. In each town, find a man of peace and stay with him, eating and drinking whatever is provided, and give him God's blessing. If you are ever unwelcomed, make a public and symbolic shaking off the dust from your sandals, abandoning them to their own fate."

Matthias was pleased when Jesus paired him with His closest disciple John. And despite the "lambs among wolves" warning, they had a safe, positive, and life-changing trip.

Upon their return, Matthias was so excited about the results of the journey, he said to Jesus in front of the others, "Master, we had a great trip. Even the demons obeyed us when we used Your name!"

Jesus replied, "I saw Satan fall from heaven like lightning. I have given you authority over all the power of the enemy ... But don't rejoice in what you can do for God. Rejoice in what God has done for you." (Luke 10:18–20 The Message)

All the way back home, Matthias contemplated what Jesus had said. Even though Jesus had not accompanied them, He was there all the time in a spiritual sense as the Good Shepherd and was aware of the spiritual battle that was ensuing. Matthias sensed that a day was soon coming when Satan would be defeated and ultimately someday destroyed. In the meantime, he would make every effort to continue to live like a "lamb among the wolves."

He never stopped praying daily that the Lord of the harvest would send out more workers into His harvest fields. And he continually rejoiced in what God had done for him through following His Son, Jesus.

The story above is my paraphrased and imaginary expansion of Luke 10:1–20. If you study the preceding context, you will see that in Luke 9, Jesus sent out just the twelve disciples on a similar mission. Matthew's parallel account says they were sent out only to the Jewish people, the "house of Israel."

This second sending out of a larger group in Luke 10 to all the Jewish and Gentile places Jesus would later visit Himself has one additional aspect mentioned that is not in Luke 9. Jesus added, "I am sending you out as lambs among wolves!" (Luke 10:3).

Author John Teter writes,

Clearly the Lord used this animal-kingdom metaphor to show a lesser and dominant pairing. The sheep are vulnerable because they don't have the predatory nature of the wolf; they aren't as cunning and crafty in their hunting and defense, and they are outnumbered. Enemies surround them, enemies that want to hurt, maim, and devour ...Without the shepherd standing with the sheep, protecting the sheep with the rod and staff and strategically moving them, they are vulnerable.[3]

Matthew's parallel account of the twelve disciples being sent out has similar imagery and adds: "So be as shrewd as snakes and harmless as doves" (Matthew 10:16). Then Jesus went on in Matthew 10 to describe the coming persecution they could expect, but He also promised that the Holy Spirit would be there to provide whatever was needed for their ministry and success.

A snake perceives sound by vibrations, always has its eyes open, and averts danger by concealment. Doves are known for their commitment to home and family and do not pick fights with others.

Dr Martin Luther King Jr using this text preached one of his more celebrated sermons titled, "A Tough Mind and a Tender Heart." He began it by saying, "Life at its best is a creative synthesis of opposites in fruitful harmony." Regarding the tough mind, he preached it was characterized by incisive thinking, realistic appraisal, and decisive judgement:

> The tough mind is sharp and penetrating, breaking through the crusts of legend and myths and sifting the true from the false. The tough-minded individual is astute and discerning. He or she has a strong, austere quality that makes for firmness of purpose and solidity of commitment.[4]

Dr King then said we need more than just cultivating a tough mind. "The gospel also demands a tender heart. Toughmindedness without tenderheartedness is cold and detached, leaving one's life in a perpetual winter devoid of the warmth of spring and the gentle heat of summer."[5] Having both of these opposites, he added, enables us to oppose injustice yet still love the perpetrators of the injustice. And he modelled that in his own life and leadership using a non-violence platform.

Nineteenth-century pastor Charles Simeon gave this interesting comment on the serpent and dove imagery: "Now the wisdom of the one and the harmlessness of the other are very desirable to be combined in the Christian character; because it is by such a union only that the Christian will be enabled to cope successfully with his more powerful enemies."[6]

Jesus was not proposing that His followers are to be weak, passive, or fearful. Nor are they to avoid actively defending religious freedoms or oppose tyranny. Rather they are to be wise, shrewd, and cunning as well as harmless and non-violent. You are possibly asking; how do you live this way in our modern day and age?

We will make a considerable effort in answering this question biblically as well as practically. But the very first question to assess is: Are we Western followers of Jesus actually living in a twenty-first-century world of wolves?

2

A WORLD OF WOLVES

The present stage of history and the
character of the advanced modern world
have combined to throw down a gauntlet
before the church in the West that is as
decisive as Rome's demand that Christians
offer incense to Caesar as lord.

Os Guinness

Kelvin Cochran overcame a difficult childhood. He worked hard as an African American to develop skills and a career that enabled him to ultimately become the fire chief of the city of Atlanta at the beginning of 2008. The next year, U.S. President Barack Obama appointed him as the United States Fire Administrator.[7]

His career ended abruptly in January 2015 when he was terminated by the city of Atlanta for expressing his Bible-based beliefs about marriage and sexuality in a self-published book he wrote encouraging Christian men from his Bible study group in the faith. Despite withering criticism and scrutiny by the media and others, he has proven to be the very personification of grace under fire. Three years later, a federal court ruled that Cochran's firing was unconstitutional. John Stonestreet, in a "Breakpoint" blog about Kelvin's treatment, concluded, "In a just and sane world, Kelvin Cochran would not have had to endure what he has endured."[8]

Our Western culture is changing quickly. Dr Jordan Peterson emerged onto the media scene as a superstar with his conservative views expressed in his book *12 Rules to Live By: An Antidote to Chaos*. Though he does not openly claim to be a follower of Jesus, he is having an incredible impact in challenging young people to read the Bible. In his best-selling book, he posits that we are now in a time of unprecedented change: family structures are collapsing, education is degenerating into indoctrination, and political society is dangerously polarizing.[9]

We are indeed seeing an increasing polarization all over the Western world today, not just in politics, racial issues, and worldviews, but also in our everyday faith lifestyle and the culture's reaction to it. Unfortunately, in my experience, our "Christian" public response to the world around us—especially on social media—has often been angry and at times even outrageous. Ed Stetzer says, "Facebook is a cesspool of conspiracy theories, straw-man arguments, and schoolyard bullying. We have reached the point where the comment sections of major newspapers are a greater testament to the depravity of man than all the theology of the Reformers put together. Many publishers have removed comments from below their online articles so the vitriol will end."[10] Unfortunately, some Christians have been influenced by this cultural degradation.

Journalist/pastor John S. Dickerson has written a very worthwhile read about how we need to stand strong in what is now a post-truth and post-Christian culture. We will look later at his significant nine-point Manifesto to counter nine major trends impacting our culture. Dickerson writes that "Christianity has undeniably failed to retain its own and has lost its influence on American culture. The percentage of young Americans abandoning the faith continues to increase dramatically with each new generation since the 1980s and the blood loss is on course to continue."[11]

In this post-truth and post-Christian ideology era, secularist gatekeepers in academia and the media actively stigmatize those who hold views different from their own. Thus, committed followers of Jesus are demonized and marginalized because we don't think and believe the same way as they do. Tolerance, by whatever definition, is suddenly no longer applicable.

In western and conservative Canada, a public school board in the province of Alberta ruled that certain passages of the Bible cannot be read or taught in Cornerstone Christian Academy (a private school within their jurisdiction) because they contain hate speech! The board chair is a strong anti-Christian. She went through the Bible with a yellow highlighter noting the passages that may not be read or studied in this Christian private school. She is especially offended by the words of the Apostle Paul in 1 Corinthians 6:9–10:

Do you not know that wrongdoers will not inherit the kingdom of God? Do not be deceived: Neither the sexually immoral nor idolaters nor adulterers nor men who have sex with men nor thieves nor the greedy nor drunkards nor slanderers nor swindlers will inherit the kingdom of God. (NIV)

The Battle River School Division board agreed with her and made the ruling official so a religious freedom case ensued against that school board. The school board officially cut ties with Cornerstone in the face of the legal challenge from the Parents Association that runs the school on the grounds of religious freedom.

The board voted overwhelmingly to close Cornerstone Christian Academy, despite telling *Global News* that the Bible verse controversy had eventually been dealt with. The parents had a plan—reopen as a completely private school.[12]

In the UK, a Christian medical doctor, David Mackereth, with thirty years of experience, lost his job after saying he could not call a man "Mrs." or "she." He then lost his case with the Employment Tribunal even though he was assisted by the Christian Legal Centre. His lawyer said the Christian doctor's belief rested on Genesis 1:27: "God created human beings in his own image. In the image of God he created them; male and female he created them." But the Tribunal ruled "*belief* in Genesis 1:27, *lack of belief* in transgenderism and conscientious objection to transgenderism in our judgment are incompatible with human dignity and conflict with the fundamental rights of others"[13] (emphasis mine).

Dr Mackereth responded that the ruling undermined his freedom of speech and freedom of thought. His legal counsel said, "The truth about mankind being made male and female is repeated throughout the Bible, including by Jesus Christ himself … People who suffer from gender dysphoria must be treated lovingly, but not telling the truth to these vulnerable people is unloving."[14]

The culture of Western nations is indeed moving further and further away from biblical morality. And it sometimes feels as though we are powerless to do anything about it. The speed at which the sexual revolution has rewritten right and wrong is breathtaking. But we have by no means seen the end of our culture's decline. Mainstream TV anchor Bill Maher openly says on national television "Religion must die!" A Canadian talk radio host described followers of Jesus as "the scum of the earth" because of our exclusive views on Jesus as the only way to heaven. And social media have become modern-day "outrage amplifiers" for the minority who are so opposed to the gospel and its proponents.

This is just the tip of the iceberg on the slippery slope followers of Jesus in our society are experiencing. And several notable Christian authors in the United States are speaking out about this situation of the marginalized church and Christian community.

In her book, *It's Dangerous to Believe*, Mary Eberstadt documents case after case of a toxic new force now hurtling across the United States and other advanced societies. One American religion professor recently assessed committed followers of Jesus as "dangerous." We are followers of a frightening faith![15]

K.A. Ellis wrote a column in *Christianity Today* magazine titled "Are US Christians Really 'Persecuted'?" She says that she usually avoids the "p" word for USA experiences because of the terrible persecution of Christians overseas.

"But," she concludes,

listen to a Middle Eastern underground house church leader: "Persecution is easier to understand when it's physical: torture, death, imprisonment ... American persecution is like an advanced stage of cancer; it eats away at you, yet you cannot feel it. This is the worst kind of persecution."

A Syrian citizen remaining in the region to assist Christians and Muslims cautions, "It wasn't only ISIS who laid waste to the church; our culture compromises with the government and our divisions against each other brewed for a long time. We are Damascus, the seat of Christianity; what happened to us can happen to you. Be careful."

When persecuted Christian leaders overseas warn about how seriously US Christians are marginalized, it's time to listen.[16]

The former president of the well-known Moody Bible Institute and Theological Seminary, J. Paul Nyquist, warns in his excellent book, *Prepare*, "Get ready. An exciting yet terrifying era is beginning for American believers. As cultural changes sweep our country, we'll soon be challenged to live out what the Bible says about confronting and responding to persecution."[17]

American conservative writer Rod Dreher says,

We are fighting for the right simply to practice our religion without being punished by the state and by the culture. And it's a fight we're losing, quite frankly ... If we want to survive, we have to return to the roots of our faith, both in thought and practice. We are going to have to learn habits of the heart forgotten by believers in the West.[18]

He thinks what we are witnessing is not just a mere moral slip, but a fundamental and long-term shift away from Christian "cosmology," or ultimate meaning. But he adds that in this fight it also becomes easier to tell who is a Christian and who is not. Rod Dreher has authored a thoughtful book on his perspective of the resulting actions Christians should take. He calls it *The Benedict Option: A Strategy for Christians in a Post-Christian Nation*.[19] I was privileged to be asked to read and evaluate this book before its final publication.

Highly respected American Bible teaching media pastor Dr David Jeremiah wrote a book that attracted much attention—*Is This the End?* In a previous publication, he shared the following critical issues which threaten the moral fabric of Western society today:

- Atheists have become angry and loud.
- Christians don't know we are in a spiritual battle.
- Jesus is publicly profaned.
- Marriage is deemed obsolete.
- Morality is in a free fall.
- The Bible is marginalized.
- The church has become irrelevant.
- An Islamic Republic can intimidate the world.[20]

Dr Jeremiah writes,

In the last few years, an increasing number of churches, businesses, and individuals have come under legal attack for standing on their biblical principles. These attacks have mostly been generated when Christians have resisted the decay of biblical sexual-moral standards in the U.S. … Jesus scolded the Pharisees for their inability to discern the signs of the times in their day (Matthew 16:3). The signs of *our* times could not be more clear: America is growing increasingly hostile toward biblical Christianity. The Bible is no longer America's moral compass. Those who hold to biblical principles are cited as intolerant at best and lawbreakers at worst.[21]

Franklin Graham has also publicly voiced this view. "I believe the end is coming," said the president of the Billy Graham Evangelistic Association. "I believe we are in the midnight hour … you see how quickly our country is deteriorating … we have seen that it has taken like a nosedive off of the moral diving board into the cesspool of humanity."[22]

Well-known football quarterback Drew Brees was part of a Focus on the Family video promoting "Take Your Bible to School Day" in September 2019. He was criticized by the media for supporting such an anti-gay organization. Focus President Jim Daly responded that they respect all people but when disagreeing with opposite opinions, they are maligned as a hate group. The LGBTQ+ magazine *OUT*, in an editorial about this controversy, shared the following:

Nobody is accusing Focus on the Family of being a hate group because of their opinions. They're a hate group because they spend millions of dollars every year to inflict pain on LGBTQ+ people and their families, whether it's through so-called "conversity [*sic*] therapy," legislation that prevents LGBTQ+ families from thriving, or the advice littered all over their website that parents should reject their gay children.

Let's be clear about what the group stands for: They worked to oppose marriage equality. They believe that same-sex couples are unfit to be parents. They called trans people "mentally ill." They oppose job protections for queer people.

It's impossible to argue with a straight face that Focus on the Family is anything but a hate group. If Daly doesn't want his organization to be called a "hate group," there's a simple solution: Stop behaving hatefully. Instead in his new video, he laments, "if you simply say, 'We believe in the biblical definition of marriage—one man and one woman'—some-how they perceive that as being hateful."[23]

The modern world's perception of our position is that we "hate" them and perceive them as hating us. Therefore, those espousing the biblical message and beliefs are worthy of being shut down, shut up, and shut out. As our postmodern and post-Christian culture devolves, the wolves will only get bigger, stronger, and more dangerous.

In his November 7, 2017, blog, Dr Michael Brown wrote:

The darkness hates the light, and this is an age-old battle that will continue until Jesus returns. To the extent we stand for sexual purity and biblical morality, and to the extent we preach Jesus as the only true way to God, we will be mocked and scorned.

That's the way it has always been, and that's the way it will always be, and that's why we must not deceive ourselves in terms of the cultural climate in America. The hostility against us is reaching a crescendo, and things could get even uglier in the days ahead … So, we can expect more abuse in the coming days. We can also expect some of our abusers to have a change of heart as they encounter the God whom they mock.[24]

Dr Brown went on to say that Peter and Paul warned us about this in the New Testament and shares how we are to live in such an environment. We will look more closely at these principles in chapter 6.

Francis Schaeffer's last major writing contribution to the Christian community in the mid-1970s was a significant volume titled *How Should We Then Live?*[25] He accurately predicted that personal peace and affluence would be the bane of the Western church by the end of the twentieth century, which would weaken our influence within the diminishing Christian culture.

The next generation's noteworthy Christian writer, Charles Colson, also wrote a treatise at the turn of this century titled *How Now Shall We Live?*[26] in which he postulates that in an era of academic attack and moral decline, true Christianity is a framework for understanding all of reality—a worldview. His solution to the downward slide of modern culture is living a fulfilling Christian life built on and reflecting biblical principles.

Both of these notable Christian communicators have passed on to their eternal reward. Yet today the Western church seems to still react with surprise at the increased attacks on our faith and the moral decline of our culture. We can become so overwhelmed by what we see as problems that we forget Jesus clearly taught us that this would happen and, even more importantly, how we are to respond to such challenges and attacks.

One of my favorite contemporary Christian authors and social critics, Os Guinness, in his book *Impossible People*, stated that we had not yet reached the tipping point of no return in 2016. His assessment was that

the present stage of history and the character of the advanced modern world have combined to throw down a gauntlet before the church in the West that is as decisive as Rome's demand that Christians offer incense to Caesar as lord … and it must be answered with a courageous *no* to everything that contradicts the call of our Lord—whatever the cost and whatever the outcome.[27]

Metaphorically, Guinness said, we are in the Thursday evening of Holy Week and the cock has not yet crowed. What is needed, he concludes, is followers of Christ who are willing to face reality without flinching and respond with a faithfulness that is unwavering. He describes these Christians as "impossible people," those who have "hearts that can melt with compassion, but with faces like flint and backbones of steel who are unmanipulable, unbribable, undeterrable, and unclubbable, without ever losing the gentleness, the mercy, the grace and the compassion of our Lord."[28]

Guinness argues that we must engage secularism and atheism in new ways, confronting competing ideas with discernment and fresh articulation of the faith. Christians are called to be "impossible people," full of courage and mercy in challenging times.

Most contemporary Christian writers have concluded that the tipping point has now been reached, and since we have lost the culture wars, we are in a condition of deciding how we should then live in the 2020s and beyond in this world of wolves.

Joseph Callahan writing in the *Huffington Post* about "The American War on Christians," concluded with these words:

Jesus said, *"In the world you shall have tribulation: but be of good cheer"* (John 16:33 NKJV), and the Apostle Peter said, *"If you suffer as a Christian, do not be ashamed, but praise God that you bear that name"* (1 Peter 4:16 NIV). So, not only should Christians expect persecution, but they should embrace it as a way to glorify God and be more Christ-like. The last thing they should ever do is complain. *"Give thanks in all circumstances; for this is the will of God in Christ Jesus for you"* (1 Thessalonians 5:18 ESV).[29]

Let's now examine how key personalities in the Bible actually did this.

3

A LAMB'S RADICALLY
DIFFERENT LIFESTYLE

In the end, we don't need grace or truth.
We need grace and truth. And for
people to see Jesus in us,
they must see both.

Randy Alcorn

When Pastor David Platt was near completion of his first book, his agent was visiting and took a telephone call from the man known as "God's smuggler," Brother Andrew in Holland. Dr Platt also spoke with Brother Andrew on the phone and asked him what he would do differently if he were to live his life over again. Brother Andrew reportedly replied, "I would be more radical! Not fanatical, but radical!"

He then quickly added, "The only gospel that many people will ever see or hear, is the gospel according to you!" David Platt wisely challenged us in his excellent best-selling book *Radical* to stop chasing after the American dream but rather live a biblically radical life of discipleship in following Jesus.[30]

Brother Andrew recently passed away at age ninety-four. Among the many sayings he was known for was "We only really believe what we are willing to die for" and "When we have an enemy image of any political or religious group or nation, the love of God cannot reach us to call us to do something about it." My favorite was, "Don't say 'Take care.' Say 'Take risks.'"

Brother Andrew was my leader, friend, and role model. I worked with him and his organization, Open Doors, for thirty-eight years. He was convinced that the essence of discipleship is your willingness to always say yes to God whenever He directs through His Holy Spirit.

Radio preacher Alistair Begg has insightfully analysed our contemporary culture as encouraging us to be "horribly opinionated, selfishly ambitious, and perniciously aggressive." I have not seen or heard a better analysis of the culture in which we live. Pastor Begg concluded that as biblical Christians, we need to live a lifestyle radically different from the culture.[31] A radically different Christian lifestyle must be biblically based. And in this and the following chapters, we will look at scriptural examples and teaching.

JOSEPH

We begin in the first book of the Bible with the life of Joseph. His life shows us that countercultural radical living was a choice that he made repeatedly. Though he seemed to be Jacob's spoiled son, he had a firm faith and trust in his father's God. As a teenager, his jealous brothers betrayed him and sold him via traders to Potiphar in the foreign land of Egypt. Joseph didn't sulk or complain. He responded to this by serving his new earthly master with excellence so that he was given complete control of all his master's household.

Then Potiphar's wife betrayed him, and he was put in prison. No self-pity or anger for Joseph about his innocence. He chose to serve the prison guards with excellence so that he was ultimately made the head administrator of the prison. He had so much integrity that he was entrusted with the cell keys and put in charge of all the other prisoners.

He was later forgotten for two whole years by the cupbearer, whose dream he interpreted, yet he showed no bitterness or impatience. And when he was finally able to tell Pharaoh his dreams and what they meant, he served the king and the people of Egypt with excellence so that he became the second most powerful person in the kingdom.

When his brothers showed up, he didn't take revenge on them. In fact, he gave them the opportunity to move to Egypt and be spared from the deadly famine. After their father Jacob died and was buried with his fathers, Joseph's brothers were now afraid that he would retaliate and get even with them. They sent him a message asking forgiveness—and Joseph wept. He said to them, "Don't be afraid of me. Am I God that I can punish you? You intended to harm me, but God intended it all for good" (Genesis 50:19–20). And Joseph reassured them by speaking kindly to them.

What countercultural characteristics do we see in Joseph? So many that it would take a whole book to itemize and explain them all. Bible scholars consider Joseph to be the ultimate foreshadowing of a Christlike character. Here are some very obvious characteristics:

- faith and trust in God to bring justice to his cause and to others
- awareness that God was willing to give him wisdom and insight
- patience to persevere in waiting for God's timing
- humility and integrity (shown by his willingness to work with excellence for pagan foreigners even when unjustly treated)
- awareness that suffering is not always bad
- ability to forgive those who severely hurt him
- an attitude of love, grace, and kindness toward his sinful brothers.

Whenever we are unjustly treated by the wolves or are in times of crisis or temptation, we should remember Joseph!

DANIEL

There are many things we must be cognizant of when we look at the life of Daniel. This is because we usually remember him only for the lion's den experience, and we often overlook the fact that he was taken captive from a home of nobility as a teenager by a foreign pagan conquering army.

Once he arrived in Babylon, the foreign country, they changed his name to one of their pagan gods and forced him to learn their language and study their literature. He and his friends were required to take part in a three-year cultural leadership training program. To avoid eating food dedicated to an idol or not kosher, he graciously suggested to his manager a creative alternative, a vegetarian diet that worked for him and his three Hebrew friends.

The pagan king was deeply impressed by the four young men and gave them top leadership roles of responsibility. They did not refuse but served with excellence. When the king was going to execute his wise counsellors for their inability to meet his impossible demands, Daniel, a man of prayer, asked God for wisdom to know and interpret the king's dream. The pagan wise men's lives were spared.

When his three God-fearing friends repeatedly refused to bow to the king's ninety-foot gold statue of himself, they humbly accepted their punishment, telling the king that their God could rescue them. But even if He didn't, they would not bow down to this idol. We learn that God did miraculously rescue them, and in addition, with them in the extremely hot furnace was a fourth man who "looked like a god," according to the king.

Daniel was so characterized by integrity in his leadership role that he made other pagan leaders jealous. This prompted them to try and defeat him through legal means, since they could find no moral fault in him to exploit. They pushed the king to create laws to counter Daniel's custom of praying three times a day. Daniel would not stop praying to his God and ended up in the lion's den, where God miraculously protected him. He lived his entire long life in captivity, humbly serving pagan leaders.

When you carefully study the first six chapters of Daniel, you quickly learn about the courage needed to not just survive but even thrive in a foreign or antagonistic culture. Dr Barry Black, the chaplain of the US Senate, says that living as a hostage in a foreign land, Daniel's life shows how we all can live with "predictable holiness."[32]

Os Guinness points out this type of courage in his book, *Impossible People.*

Are we [in the West] showing that we too are prepared to follow Jesus and his authority at any cost? When an imperceptible bow would have saved Daniel's three friends, they defied King Nebuchadnezzar's idolatry at the threat of being burned alive. When simply closing a window and drawing his curtains could have saved Daniel himself, he chose to risk the lions rather than mute his allegiance to God.[33]

What countercultural characteristics do we see in Daniel?

• conviction that God's Word and ways are right
• calm and courage when under fire
• confidence in his God who holds the future
• courtesy and respect paid to everyone
• an entire lifetime of integrity
• willingness to sacrifice himself for godly principles
• constant communication with God through prayer
• his openness as a humble servant of foreign godless leaders

Whenever we are under pressure to compromise our faith and practice, or fearful of the wolves, we should remember Daniel (and his friends)!

ESTHER

Queen Esther, a Jewish exile in Persia, like Daniel, is probably best remembered as a beautiful woman who took a great risk and became a hero to her nation. She was willing to say "Yes!" to a request that she take action on behalf of her people, which would require her to risk her very life.

Esther was orphaned as a young girl and adopted by her older cousin, Mordecai, who cared for her as his own daughter. In the Persian king's search for beautiful young virgins, she was taken away from her home and Uncle Mordecai to be prepared for the king's beauty contest.

When she arrived at the palace in the citadel of Susa, she was guided by the harem keeper, Hegai, and immediately won his favor. She even won favor over all the other contestants with King Xerxes and he chose her as his new queen, not knowing she was Jewish.

The antagonist, Haman, who hated Mordecai, cunningly convinced King Xerxes to have all the Jews killed in one day. When Esther learned of this, Mordecai asked her to appeal to the king on behalf of the Jewish people. She said yes, even though in the process of doing so, she would risk her life, since the king was not approachable without an invitation. But first she wisely designed a plan. She requested her cousin to gather the Jews in Susa together to fast for three days, and she and her maids would do the same. She said, "then, though it is against the law, I will go in to see the king. If I must die, I must die" (Esther 4:16).

Mordecai had reminded her, "Who knows if perhaps you were made queen for just such a time as this?" (Esther 4:14).

On the third day of her fast, Esther put on her royal robes and stood at the entrance of King Xerxes's hall. I suspect her heart was pounding. He held out his gold scepter, the sign that she could approach the throne, and then he offered her whatever she wanted—as much as half of the kingdom. She simply asked him to be her guest, along with Haman, at a banquet that night. Esther displayed patience and calm under immense pressure.

They all had a good time at the banquet, and Esther invited them back the following night. Haman was in great spirits, having been invited twice to dinner with the king and queen. That night, after the first banquet, the king could not sleep and called for the chronicles of his reign, where he read that Mordecai had earlier alerted him to an assassination plot.

In an amazing twist of plot, the king required Haman to royally parade Mordecai—the very person that Haman wanted to kill—through the city streets with praise. Haman arrived at the second banquet to hear Esther ask the king to spare her life and the lives of her Jewish people destined for annihilation by their enemy, Haman. Haman was subsequently impaled on a pole he had set up for Mordecai, and a detailed plan was put in place that would spare Esther's life and her Jewish people from the earlier death edict of the king initiated by Haman.

She must have been a very gracious person! To repeatedly win the king's favor required much more than just outward beauty. The way she dealt with Haman, the enemy of Mordecai and the Jewish people, was very bold. Her dinner plans and her patience resulted in justice being accomplished and the lives of her people spared from genocide. As so often happened in Bible times, and even today, God empowered an obedient person in a negative situation to turn it into good.

Despite the disadvantages of her nationality, her gender (in a patriarchal era), and the king's restrictive access laws, Esther rose above her circumstances to accomplish a great victory. To this day, Esther's faith, favor, and courage are remembered among her people in the annual Feast of Purim.

What countercultural characteristics do we see in the life of Esther?

- She won favor with everyone she met and with whom she connected.
- Her first response to her desperate plight was to call for communal fasting before she acted.
- She believed and accepted her cousin's assessment that she might have come to her position in the kingdom for just this purpose of saving her people.
- She designed a plan that required courage and inspired hope.
- She took a great risk on behalf of her people, which required faith, patience, and wisdom, without knowing the outcome beforehand.
- She faced her fears and put the needs of others ahead of her own life.
- She was enabled by God to be an overcomer—over disadvantages, limitations, and circumstances.

Whenever we are tempted to shrink back from a life-threatening decision and action requiring grace and boldness, we should remember Esther.

JEREMIAH

God called Jeremiah to warn the kingdom of Judah of its impending destruction and promised to protect him. His life spanned the reigns of five kings of Judah. The personal difficulties and struggles he encountered as he delivered God's messages (described in the books of Jeremiah and Lamentations) have prompted scholars to refer to him as "the weeping prophet." It seemed that no one listened to him and his messages from God. Yet he faithfully, persistently, and obediently shared the truth that God had given him.

While Joseph and Daniel lived counterculturally among wolves in a foreign land, Jeremiah was called to stand up to the wolves who were his own people and culture in his own country and city. God's disgust with His chosen people was that they had left their love for Him and gone after other gods.

To the leaders of the land, He identified through Jeremiah's messages the lifestyle He wanted them to abandon: quit their evil deeds; stop mistreating foreigners, widows and orphans; stop murdering the innocent. On the other hand, there was a lifestyle He wanted them to adopt: be fair-minded and just; do what was right; rescue from their oppressors those who had been robbed (Jeremiah 22:3).

In his initial calling from God to become a prophet, Jeremiah, who worried about his youthfulness, received specific instruction to not be afraid of people. As you read the story of his life, it is obvious that God was preparing him.

Jeremiah's ministry prompted plots against him. Unhappy with his message, his priestly kin and the men of Anathoth conspired to kill him. However, the Lord revealed the conspiracy to Jeremiah, protected his life, and declared disaster for the men of Anathoth. When Jeremiah complained to the Lord about this persecution, he was told that the attacks on him would only become worse (Jeremiah 11:18–12:6).

A temple official in Jerusalem named Pashur had Jeremiah beaten and put in the stocks at the Upper Gate of Benjamin at the temple for a day. After this, Jeremiah expressed lament over the difficulty that speaking God's Word had caused him and regretted becoming a laughingstock and the target of mockery; yet he concluded that Jehovah's words burned like a fire in his heart and bones.

At the beginning of Nebuchadnezzar's second siege of Jerusalem, Jeremiah offered his people a choice of life or death. People who stayed in the city would die and those who surrendered to the Babylonians would live. Few chose to live.

God then sent Jeremiah to the courtyard in front of the Temple to proclaim that if the people did not listen to the Lord, He would destroy the Temple as He destroyed Shiloh where the Tabernacle was located. And God would also make Jerusalem an object of cursing in every nation on earth (26:6).

After hearing this message, everyone mobbed and threatened him, shouting, "Kill him!" Officials from the palace rushed over to hold court. Jeremiah calmly responded to the charges against him, "Do with me as you think best" (26:14). Ahikam persuaded the court not to turn Jeremiah over to the mob to be killed.

The biblical narrative portrays Jeremiah as being subject to additional persecutions. Because of his prophecies of the enemy's success, the king's officials took Jeremiah and put him into a cistern, where he sank down into the mud. The intent seemed to be to kill Jeremiah by allowing him to starve to death in a manner designed to allow the officials to claim to be innocent of his blood. A foreigner rescued Jeremiah by pulling him out of the cistern, but Jeremiah remained imprisoned until Jerusalem fell to the Babylonian army in 587 BC.

The conquering Babylonian general allowed him to stay with Gedaliah, the newly appointed governor of Judah. Johanan, Gedaliah's successor, rejected Jeremiah's counsel. He fled to Egypt, taking with him Jeremiah and Baruch, Jeremiah's faithful scribe and servant, as well as the king's daughters. There, the prophet probably spent the remainder of his life, still seeking in vain to turn the people to God, against whom they had so long rebelled.

In all the negativity of his message, Jeremiah felt a deep solidarity with his people. He let us see his heart as he struggled to obey God. And he was quick to prophesy good news whenever God gave it, especially the news that God would bring His people back to their land. In the meantime, they were to work for the peace and prosperity of the foreign city in which they lived (for seventy years) and the news that God would make a new covenant with His people that would not be written in stone but on their hearts.

What countercultural characteristics do we see in Jeremiah? Although it seemed few listened to his warnings and changed their ways, he:

- repeatedly and boldly declared God's messages of judgement without fear of retaliation.
- trusted and appealed to God for his safety even when circumstances looked bad.

- persevered in his faithfulness to God through much opposition.
- creatively shared God's messages in writing when oral delivery was impossible.
- displayed optimism and God's love for His people amid the messages of judgement.
- courageously kept his confidence in God's promise to ultimately bring His people back.
- positively predicted hope: a coming Messiah and a New Covenant with Israel.

Whenever we are tempted to not speak the truth in love or to give up under pressure, we should remember Jeremiah!

MARY

Every time Mary, the mother of Jesus, is mentioned in the Bible there is a significant and respectful point being made about her. She first emerges as a young woman (most think she was likely still a teenager).

When she was surprised and fearful at the appearance of the angel Gabriel, she was told not to be afraid. And that fearlessness seems to characterize the rest of her life. She was bold enough to question an angel as to how her predicted pregnancy could possibly happen since she was a virgin. Once the plan of God was explained to her, she then boldly responded, "I am the Lord's servant. May everything you have said about me come true" (Luke 1:38). This was a very brave statement in light of her knowing that her fiancé could divorce her as a result. And her community could stigmatize her for a baby born out of wedlock.

The next scene is her visit to her elderly cousin Elizabeth who also was experiencing a miraculous pregnancy. Under the influence of the Holy Spirit, Elizabeth started the tradition of calling Mary "blessed among women, mother of my Lord." She also declared, "You are blessed because you believed that the Lord would do what he had said" (Luke 1:45).

Mary responded with a powerful song of praise to the Lord we call the Magnificat. Mary's response during a life-changing moment is wonderful, almost incredible. At a dark time in Israel, she was able to see the hope of the Messiah. She proclaimed that her spirit rejoiced in God even in uncertainty and despair.

We then learn that she joined Joseph, her fiancé, on the long journey from Nazareth to Bethlehem, where she humbly delivered her baby boy in a stable manger. It appears there was no more room in their family's guest area. Shepherds came from the fields after the dramatic announcement by angels and then told everyone what had happened. "Mary kept all these things in her heart and thought about them often" (Luke 2:19).

She learned more about the uniqueness of her son when, aged twelve, He disappeared on their return home from the Passover celebrations in Jerusalem. They searched frantically for Him until He was located talking to the religious teachers in the Temple. He explained, "Didn't you know that I must be in my Father's house? (Luke 2:49). Luke says His parents didn't understand what He meant.

The first sign of His glory for Jesus occurred at a wedding in Cana to which His family was invited. Mary, His mother, came to Him to share the embarrassment of the wedding hosts that they had run out of wine. He seemed to put her off by declaring that His time had not yet come. By now, Mary must have realized His giftings and powers because she told the household servants, "Do whatever he tells you" (John 2:5). And Jesus turned water into wine, which ultimately turned potential wedding embarrassment into praise.

After a few appearances in Jesus' ministry years, Mary was seen at the cross and then the tomb. She was central to the last moments before He died and an early witness to His resurrection. As her eldest son, Jesus gave her care to His best friend, John, from the cross. Tradition says John cared for her until her death, first in Jerusalem and later in Ephesus.

In Acts chapter 1, she is mentioned as present in the upper room with the apostles. She remained part of the church community waiting for the Holy Spirit. Her last biblical mention is in verse 14. "They all met together and were constantly united in prayer, along with Mary the mother of Jesus, several other women, and the brothers of Jesus" (Acts 1:14).

In her book *Women In The Bible Small Group Bible Study*, Marina Hofman makes this insightful comment:

As a witness to the risen Christ, Mary testifies to the resurrection. Remarkably, even after Jesus ascends to heaven, Mary continues to do God's work, waiting for the Holy Spirit alongside the apostles. As favored by God as Mary is, she still waits for even more of what God has for her. By the time of the ascension, Mary's mission to bring Christ into the world is complete. But she is committed to the lifelong mission of bringing Jesus to all the world, and so she continues to spread the salvation message of Jesus.[34]

Although Mary was originally afraid and faced uncertainty, she trusted God's plan for her life and followed with faith, hope, and trust until the end. We can be encouraged by Mary's example. Say yes to God's plan for your life, and realize that He will strengthen you and provide guidance and support.

What countercultural characteristics do we see in the life of Mary?

- She was "full of grace and favor."
- Overcoming her fears, she became a "blessed" person.
- She was prayerful, hopeful, and humble.
- Willingly she said yes to God in spite of many questions.
- Through the Magnificat, Mary encourages us to examine our response to life-changing situations.
- She rejoiced even in uncertainty and despair.
- Mary practiced a lifelong commitment to God's calling and God's community.

Whenever we are fearful and unsure of what the future holds, we should remember Mary.

JESUS

In the New Testament, we are quickly introduced to the God-man, Jesus of Nazareth. This puts Him in a category of His own, but we are repeatedly encouraged in Scripture to be conformed to His character and lifestyle. He called Himself the Good Shepherd. He knows each sheep by name, He leads them in and out, they listen to His voice and not to the voice of a stranger, He feeds them with good things, and He lays down his life for them (John 10). When one is missing, He leaves all those other sheep standing around in the field and goes off to find the lost one (Luke 15:3–7). Ultimately, as Isaiah foretold, "He was led like a lamb to the slaughter" (Isaiah 53:7).

Again, a whole book could not exhaust the character qualities of Jesus, the Good Shepherd, but here are some key characteristics of how He lived counterculturally.

FULL OF GRACE AND TRUTH

The first character description of Jesus, the Logos, is in the prologue of John's Gospel when he shares that Jesus left heaven's glory and took on humanity "pitching his tent" to live among us to reveal the Father to us. "We have seen his glory, the glory of the one and only Son, who came from the Father, full of *grace and truth*" (John 1:14 NIV, emphasis mine).

Notice that both grace and truth give a balance to life, but "grace" is mentioned first. To show grace is to extend favour or kindness to one who doesn't deserve it and can never earn it. Receiving God's acceptance by grace always stands in sharp contrast to earning it based on works. Every time the mention of grace appears, there is the idea of its being undeserved. In no way is the recipient getting what he or she deserves. Favor is being extended simply out of the goodness of the giver's heart.

Also, grace is absolutely and totally free. You will never be asked to pay it back. You couldn't even if you tried. Grace comes to us free and clear with no strings attached. It is the act of unmerited favour—most often to the down and out.

Christ came down to us from the Father in heaven, and He reminds us that the greatest in the kingdom is the one who serves. The ladder of power reaches up, and the ladder of grace reaches down. Dr Donald Barnhouse said it best: "Love that goes upward is worship; love that goes outward is affection; love that stoops is grace."

The world is truly enamoured with those whose lives exhibit grace. A TV evening news commentator was talking about the loving exchange between two women rivals at the 2019 US Tennis Open Championships. He said, "It's one thing to lose with grace, but quite another thing to win with grace!"[35]

The funeral of Queen Elizabeth II was held today as I write this. As one of the estimated four billion people who viewed the funeral on television, I heard repeatedly throughout the day that as the longest reigning British monarch, she led with grace and selfless devotion.

Jesus never used the word "grace" itself. He just taught it and lived it. And as we have seen, it was written as a description of how He lived His life. In a world of darkness and demands, rules and regulations, requirements and expectations demanded by the hypocritical religious leaders, Jesus came and ministered in a new and different way.

After commenting on His glory, John goes on to add, "Out of his fullness we have all received grace in place of grace already given" (John 1:16 NIV). John and the other chosen disciples (some reference them as apostles) became marked men. His style became theirs. They absorbed His tolerance, acceptance, love, warmth, and compassion so that it ultimately transformed their lives. They too therefore lived their lives demonstrating grace! Grace is a force stronger than vengeance, stronger than racism, stronger than hate.

In his classic book *The Grace Awakening*, Chuck Swindoll shares four practical expectations from grace in our lives.

a. A greater appreciation for God's gifts

Those who claim the freedom God offers gain an appreciation for the gifts that come with life: the free gifts of salvation, life, laughter, music, beauty, friendship and forgiveness.

b. Less time and energy being critical or concerned about others' choices

When you begin to operate in the context of grace and freedom, you become gradually less petty. You will allow others room to make their own decisions in life, even though you may choose otherwise. A grace-full follower of Jesus is one who looks at the world and others through "grace-tinted lenses."

c. More tolerance and less judgement

When you are so involved in your own pursuit of grace, you'll no longer lay guilt trips on those with whom you disagree.

d. A giant step toward maturity

As your world expands, thanks to an awakening of your understanding of grace, your maturity will enlarge. You will become more like Jesus, and you will never be the same![36]

In the world of wolves, we also need to carefully distinguish between gracious living and what we often call and like—being "nice." Author Sharon Hodde Miller writes:

I cannot follow Jesus and be nice. Not equally. Because following Jesus means following someone who spoke hard and confusing truths, who was honest with his disciples—even when it hurt— who condemned the hypocrisy of the Pharisees and turned over tables in the temple. Jesus was a man who went face-to-face with the devil himself and died on a cross rather than succumb to the status quo.

We exist in a world that swings between sweetness and outrage, two behaviors that seem to be at odds with one another. In reality, they are two sides of the same coin: a lack of spiritual formation. When our civility isn't rooted in something sturdy and deep, when our good behavior isn't springing from the core of who we are but is instead merely a mask we put on, it is only a matter of time before the façade crumbles away and our true state is revealed: an entire generation of people who are really good at looking good.

The solution, however, is not to trade in our appearance of niceness for an appearance of boldness. We have to go deeper into Christ.

Jesus was loving. He was gracious. He was forgiving. He was kind. But he was not nice. He was a man who would leave the 99 sheep to rescue the one, but he was also totally unafraid of offending people. Jesus understood the difference between graciousness and personal compromise, between speaking truth and needlessly alienating people. Rather than wear a shiny veneer, he became the embodiment of rugged love. This, not niceness, is what we are called to.[37]

As followers of Jesus in the twenty-first-century post-truth environment, we are quick to highlight that we know the truth, or that we are living by the truth, unlike others. It is sad that truth is now defined more as feelings than objective propositions. I remember as a teenager that Bishop Fulton Sheen would challenge young people on his TV program to "find truth; face truth; follow truth," on the basis that Jesus said the truth will set you free. But in our standing up for truth, we often forget that Jesus's example of "rugged love" was characterized by being full of *grace* and truth.

Why are some Jesus followers so often characterized by lack of grace—or what writer Philip Yancey calls "ungrace"—when we try to communicate truth to the pagans and wolves around us? Perhaps this is the balanced life that the pagans and wolves so desire to see. Satan has deceived us to believe we do not need grace—only truth. Our witness to a post-truth world would be so much stronger if the grace shone through while and when we are sharing what Francis Schaeffer prophetically often called the "true truth."

We also must avoid the either/or option trap that the world presents— condone or condemn. Many times, wolves use the issues to force Jesus followers intentionally to choose one of the two camps because either way they win: you either agree with the world's definition of sexual morality or you sideline yourself and your influence with angry rhetoric. When the two options given to us are to either condone (full grace) or condemn (full truth), we need to do what Jesus did: embody both grace and truth.

As Randy Alcorn points out in his book, *The Grace and Truth Paradox*, truth without grace breeds self-righteousness and crushing legalism. Grace without truth breeds deception and moral compromise. Therefore, grace without truth deceives people and ceases to be grace. Truth without grace crushes people and ceases to be truth. Alcorn says, "In the end, we don't need grace *or* truth. We need grace *and* truth. And for people to see Jesus in us, they must see both."[38]

In his benediction in 2 Corinthians 13:14, the apostle Paul gives a characteristic for each of the triune Godhead personalities. For Jesus, the Son, it is "grace."

LOVING

How can Jesus followers dispense grace in a society that is or seems to be veering away from God? Elijah hid out in caves. On the other hand, his contemporary Obadiah worked within the system, running Ahab's palace while sheltering God's prophets on the side. Joseph, Esther, and Daniel were employed by heathen empires. Jesus submitted to the judgement of a Roman governor. Paul appealed his case all the way to Caesar.

The one big thing the church has over the world is showing grace. Jesus did not let any institution interfere with His love for individuals. Here is where the fruit of the Spirit is so important in our lives. Jesus said we are to have one distinguishing mark—neither political correctness nor moral superiority, but love. *It all starts with love.* If we first don't focus on love, the rest of the characteristics will not matter (1 Corinthians 13:1): *love is the foundation.* The fact Jesus came to earth to rescue us is an example of His love. On earth, He loved everyone— especially the unlovely and the marginalized. And then He sacrificed His own life for you and me. "We love each other because he loved us first" (1 John 4:19).

FORGIVING

Another standout characteristic of Jesus is forgiveness. It is the reason we get to spend eternity in heaven with Him. He forgives us of all our sins. He even forgave those who crucified Him. If Jesus can forgive us for everything, shouldn't we model how to forgive everyone else?

I heard an elderly priest, who had been taking confessions for more than forty years, interviewed on the radio. When asked what sin most often came up in the confessions he heard, he replied, "The one that outnumbered all the others together—unwillingness to forgive." Our culture knows about forgiveness but finds it hard to practice. Yet our own forgiveness depends on it! "If you forgive those who sin against you, your heavenly Father will forgive you" (Matthew 6:14).

HUMBLE

Jesus never claimed to be someone He was not. He was God's Son. He performed miracles. He healed many … yet He never focused the attention on Himself. To the contrary, He consistently pointed people towards God the Father and constantly reminded all who could hear Him that these things too could be accomplished through faith. To practically demonstrate this characteristic of humility, He, their master, took the place of a missing servant on the night of the Last Supper and washed His disciples' feet. He then said, "You now do this too!" He gives us more grace. That is why Scripture says: "God opposes the proud but favors the humble" (James 4:6).

COMPASSIONATE

You may say, "Wait a minute! Are you talking about the same Jesus who called out the Pharisees with some strong language and angrily overturned the tables of moneychangers in the temple court?" Yes, I am, and I will deal with the topic of anger—specifically Jesus's anger—in chapter 8. Remember, our thesis is about living a "balanced" life. If these scenes were all we knew about Jesus, we might come to different conclusions.

The Jesus of the Bible never tired of helping others. In fact, it was why He came to earth, "to seek and save those who are lost" (Luke 19:10). Even when He was on a specific mission, He never hesitated to stop and help those in need. But before we can help others, we need to cultivate a heart like His for helping others.

"Instead, be kind to each other, tenderhearted, forgiving one another, just as God through Christ has forgiven you" (Ephesians 4:32).

PRAYERFUL

Prayer is pure communication with our Father in heaven. Jesus Christ prayed often for friends and enemies as well as for help during trials. "Before daybreak the next morning, Jesus got up and went out to an isolated place to pray" (Mark 1:35). We too have access to divine help and guidance through prayer. We can follow the Savior as we pray daily, expressing thanks and seeking divine assistance in our lives.

VIRTUOUS

Jesus Christ was pure and virtuous; "he faced all of the same testings we do, yet he did not sin" (Hebrews 4:15). If we are to be virtuous like the Savior in an unclean world, we must turn away from things that pollute our minds, bodies, and spirits. Carefully choosing our entertainment and actively avoiding the pervasive pornography will greatly increase our virtue and cleanliness before the Lord.

What countercultural characteristics do we see in Jesus?
- full of both *grace* and truth
- loving everyone—even the unlovely and the marginalized
- forgiving everyone—even those who crucified Him
- characterized by humility
- kind and compassionate
- an example in persistent prayer
- in every temptation, He did not sin

Whenever we are misunderstood, misquoted, misinterpreted, misjudged, misconstrued, or mistreated, we should remember Jesus!

The clarion call of Scripture and history is for followers of Jesus to respond to the challenges of their culture with courage and, as Jesus Himself exhibited, a life filled with grace and truth.

Knowing the character of Jesus and realizing the heart attitude He requires, it therefore follows to ask, what did Jesus teach us we should *do* to live counterculturally the way He did?

4

THE LAMB THAT WAS SLAIN

We overcome evil in the world, not by inflicting
more hurt, but by absorbing the hurt,
even if it costs us our lives.

Darrell Johnson

In John's vision of heaven in Revelation 5, no one was found worthy to open the scrolls, and it made John weep. Then John heard that the Lion of Judah was the only one worthy to open the scrolls. But when he looked, he didn't see a lion. He saw a Lamb that looked as if it had been slain. When the Lamb took and opened the scroll, everyone in heaven, numbering in the millions, sang praises to the Lamb.

Dr Darrell Johnson, in his brilliant book *Discipleship on the Edge*, discusses the imagery and structure of Revelation, the final book in the Bible challenging followers of Jesus to "overcome." In an appendix of the book, Dr Johnson shows how the entire document (Revelation) is structured as a chiasm—an ancient form of writing that places the central point right in the middle. That centre point is Revelation 12:11. He concludes:

There is only one way to "overcome": the way Jesus did, as a Lamb, as pictured in Revelation 5. Thus 12:11, the central verse of the whole book—"*They* [disciples of Jesus] *overcame him* [the dragon] *by the blood of the Lamb and by the word of their testimony; they did not love their lives so much as to shrink from death*" (NIV). (Emphasis original.)

The structure itself declares the message that since Jesus overcomes evil not by being a Lion who hurts others, but by being a Lamb who absorbs hurt, so too we overcome evil in the world, not by inflicting more hurt, but by absorbing the hurt, *even if it costs us our lives.* The structure itself declares the mystery that in losing our lives we actually win, "overcome," just as Jesus did.[39] (Emphasis mine.)

Please read that last paragraph again and meditate on it for a moment. The imagery and insight help us understand Jesus's teaching ministry even more clearly. Jesus repeatedly warned His followers that if the world hated Him, it would hate them also (John 15:18). In Luke's sermon on the plain, Jesus reminds His disciples that this opposition is a blessing—not a blessing we ever hear many Jesus followers praying for.

"Blessed are you when people hate you, when they exclude you and insult you and reject your name as evil, because of the Son of Man" (Luke 6:22 NIV).

So, the very basic and first element of Jesus's teaching is awareness that as a follower of Jesus, you can expect opposition, just as Jesus Himself experienced (Hebrews 12:3). He indicated that it would come from the world of wolves and possibly even from your own family and friends (see Matthew 10:21).

Jesus utilizes four strong verbs in Luke 6:22 declaring that His followers would be *hated, excluded, insulted,* and *rejected* (NIV). And in addition, He said this was a blessing! We can't forget that.

The four verbs from the NIV translation form an acrostic and we get the word HEIR from the first letters (this is coincidental in one English version):

- **H**ated
- **E**xcluded
- **I**nsulted
- **R**ejected

Seeing this reminds me of Romans 8:17, where the apostle Paul told us, "Now if we are children, then we are *heirs—heirs* of God and *co-heirs* with Christ, if indeed we *share in his sufferings* in order that we may also share in his glory" (NIV, emphasis mine). So, when we share in Jesus's sufferings (He outlined them in Luke 6:22 as hatred, exclusion, insults, and rejection) we become heirs who will also share in His glory.

The four verbs above can be experienced in varying degrees of intensity. We tend to think of opposition as only the very intense forms. But even when you experience hatred, exclusion, insults, and rejection (because of Jesus in you) in a lighter intensity, you are still being opposed. This is like one of my favorite foods—Indian curry! It can be experienced in a mild, medium, or hot form.[40]

Jesus was saying these responses occur because of our witness for Him, meaning we may lose standing with our peers and be loathed and ridiculed by powerful people and institutions, abandoned by some of our friends, called nasty names, and denied valuable professional opportunities.

Unfortunately, a psychological principle has been shown throughout history that when a victim later comes to a position of power, the victim may perpetrate the exact same actions against others that he or she suffered. Christianity has sometimes been twisted by pride into a system that can also perpetrate hate, exclusion, insults, and rejection. We "Jesus followers" have a checkered history about which we must be honest. But this is a situation not at all condoned by Jesus.

In fact, looking further in the passage to Luke 6:27–31, we see how Jesus taught us to respond to this kind of treatment mentioned in verse 22. First, He proclaimed four responses; then He gave four practical examples:

> "To you who are listening I say: Love your enemies, do good to those who hate you, bless those who curse you, pray for those who mistreat you. If someone slaps you on one cheek, turn to them the other also. If someone takes your coat, do not withhold your shirt from them. Give to everyone who asks you, and if anyone takes what belongs to you, do not demand it back. Do to others as you would have them do to you." (Luke 6:27–31 NIV)

1. **Love** your enemies.
2. **Do good** to those who hate you.
3. **Bless** those who curse you.
4. **Pray** for those who mistreat you.

Talk about countercultural living! If we only concentrated on practicing these four actions, we would already be radical. But there is more—four more detailed specific life actions!

1. **"If someone slaps you on one cheek, turn to them the other also."** When Jesus taught here about "turning the other cheek," it was an offensive— not a defensive—act of peace. In the culture of Jesus's day, a person who slapped another on the cheek normally used the back of the right hand to the right cheek

of the other as an act of insult by a superior to an inferior. Thus, by turning the "other" cheek, the person hit (the perceived powerless one) takes an initiative to force the aggressor to either back down or now return with a second blow. This time the "hit" must be with an aggressive open palm or fist, thereby transforming the nature of the relationship.

With the Christlike response of turning the other cheek, the one struck does not assume the inferior place of humiliation the striker had in mind but stands forth as an equal. The supposedly powerless person has redefined the relationship and forced the oppressor into a moral choice: escalate the violence or respond with repentance and reconciliation. Some will escalate the violence, and then you must quickly decide how you will respond. I do not believe this illustration is the basis for total pacifism. But on the other hand, no matter how you describe the meaning, Jesus is teaching a bottom line of making every effort for non-violence.

2. **"If someone takes your coat, do not withhold your shirt from them."** In a parallel passage in Matthew 5:41, Jesus says to carry a load for two miles for a person who can legally demand that you carry it for only one mile. From that we get our English idiom "go the extra mile." So it is clear that Jesus was teaching His followers not to be legalistic or stingy and only do the minimum required in a difficult situation. A disciple of Jesus will do at least twice what is demanded or expected.

The Roman occupiers were notorious in forcing service of various kinds from the occupied people. Can you imagine a Roman soldier of the day, used to the complaining and grumbling of Jewish men when they were pressed into forced service, such as being required to carry the soldier's heavy pack for a mile, when a person cheerfully says, "OK, I'll go two miles!"? And someone who might even say, "Where's your camp? I'll carry it all the way there for you!" So Jesus was really saying here, "Don't oblige—when compelled—with bitter and obvious resentment, but respond with cheerfulness and good grace."

3. **"Give to everyone who asks you, and if anyone takes what belongs to you, do not demand it back."** Here is a command that gets right to the heart of countering our innate materialism. It even challenges our Western concept of justice. The Old Testament had laid down "an eye for an eye and a tooth for a tooth," equal justice to match the crime. But Jesus said in effect, "My disciples will be giving people and not concerned only about themselves or their own

'things.'" We do not see this command practiced very much anywhere in our culture—especially the latter part of the command. Jesus was further revealing that people are more important than things.

4. **"Do to others as you would have them do to you."** We have long referred to this as "the Golden Rule." One of my atheistic university professors at graduate school said to me one day, "Jesus wasn't the first to say this." I looked it up, and the famous Rabbi, Hillel, and the Greek philosopher, Socrates, both expressed this idea, but negatively: "Do not do to others what angers you if done to you by others." Jesus turned this statement on its head and made it positive and proactive. "Do to others as you would have them do to you." Greek scholar Dr William Barclay said this is the "Everest [highest] of ethical statements ever made!" But this instruction is much easier to quote and slogan than to live!

In all of this, Jesus never suggested isolation from the world as our response to the challenges we might face. He was known as "the friend of sinners" and prayed to His Father that His followers would be "*in* the world but *not of* the world"!

Matthew included in his Sermon on the Mount (Matthew 5–7) more teachings of Jesus for those who would follow Him and live counterculturally. Peacemaking is one of those teachings. He said, "God blesses those who work for peace, for they will be called the children of God" (Matthew 5:9).

Brother Andrew, founder of Open Doors International, proposed a three-point peace plan for Christians worldwide:

First, we desire to have our Heart at Peace. We truly believe every human on earth desires to have inner peace—based on freedom from guilt and freedom from anger. We want our heart to experience forgiveness and freedom in Jesus Christ.

Second, we desire to have our Homes at Peace. We want our homes to be havens of safety—free from abuse. We want children and women to live without fear and violence—based on hope and trust in God's plan for the family.

Third, we desire to have our Community at Peace. We want our community free from fights, murders and thefts. We want communities at peace—based on love and respect for one another—regardless of ideologies or religion.[41]

Even clinical psychologist Dr Jordan Peterson has publicly declared this as true. In a recent speech at the International Convention Center in Jerusalem, he stressed that responsibility and truth begin in our individual lives and family units.

> To make peace, one first has to confront the serpent in his or her garden—a parallel to Adam and Eve. If you can bring peace to your house, then you can learn to bring peace to your community. And if you bring peace to your community, then you can make some headway in bringing peace to the world. These things start locally as far as I'm concerned. And in some sense, that's so heartening because it means you have all the possibility of the world at hand.[42]

With the possession of a meek spirit, we are equipped to step into the midst of conflict and be ambassadors waging peace that passes all understanding. The richness of the New Testament word translated "peace" describes a condition of perfect and complete positive well-being. It also describes right relationships—intimate fellowship and goodwill between human beings. Peace comes not from avoiding issues but from facing them, making peace even when the way is through trouble.

Such actions may involve laying down one's life, as Jesus did, in order to reconcile humanity with God and break down barriers among humanity (Galatians 3:26–29). Are we willing to pay the price that others might find peace with God?

Right after Jesus predicted to his disciples in Matthew 16 that He would ultimately be killed in Jerusalem (and resurrected after three days) and Peter argued with Him about it, Jesus also addressed the expected commitment of His disciples.

> Then Jesus said to his disciples, "If any of you wants to be my follower, you must turn from your selfish ways, take up your cross and follow me. If you try to hang on to your life, you will lose it. But if you give up your life for my sake, you will save it." (Matthew 16:24–25)

Taking up the cross was a direct reference to Roman execution at the time. Jesus was clearly talking about death, and not an "easy" death. Dietrich Bonhoeffer, the German theologian who gave up his life taking a stand against Hitler, wrote, "When Christ calls a man, he bids him come and die."[43] That's what it means to lose our life in order to save it. Jesus himself was our example, being willing to go to the cross on behalf of others—even a lost, disobedient world.

Sundar Singh is credited as the first missionary from India to cross the Himalayan mountains to take the gospel to Nepal and Tibet about one hundred years ago. At thirty-six years of age, he made his last trip over the mountains. He never returned and is assumed to have been a martyr for Jesus.

In his diary left behind, he had written, "It is easy to die for Christ. It is hard to live for Him. Dying takes only a few minutes—or at worst an hour or two—but to live for Christ means to die daily to myself."

When I think of some of the people I've met in years of ministry overseas, who have died to themselves daily, it makes me want to pause and tell you their stories. Let's shift gears and listen to the stories and examples of brothers and sisters who have faced the most ravenous wolves "the Jesus way" and were willing to die for Jesus. Some even lived to tell the end of their story and have been able to identify with the song written by Ray Boltz:

I pledge allegiance to the Lamb,
With all my strength, with all I am
I will seek to honor His commands
I pledge allegiance to the Lamb![44]

5
THE EXAMPLE OF OUR GLOBAL FAMILY

Comfortable conformity to the world in which we live today may be the most subtle form of Christ denial.

Richard Halverson

Kefa Sempangi was pastor of the large Redeemed Church of Uganda. On Easter Sunday 1973 was his first serious brush with death at the hands of Idi Amin's goons under "the reign of terror." After an all-day worship service, in which he preached about the suffering of Jesus and His triumph over evil and death, Kefa went exhausted to the vestry to change clothes—too exhausted to notice the five strangers (government secret police goons) following him into the room. He says:

> They stood between me and the door, pointing their rifles at my face … For a long moment no one said anything. Then the tallest man, obviously the leader, spoke. "We are going to kill you," he said. "If you have something to say, say it before you die." He spoke quietly but his face was twisted with hatred.
>
> I could only stare at him. For a sickening moment I felt the full weight of his rage. We had never met before but his deepest desire was to tear me to pieces. My mouth felt heavy and my limbs began to shake. Everything left my control. *They will not need to kill me*, I thought to myself. *I am just going to fall over dead and I will never see my family again.*

From far away I heard a voice, and I was astonished to realize that it was my own. "I do not need to plead my own cause," I heard myself saying. "I am a dead man already. My life is dead and hidden in Christ. It is your lives that are in danger, you are dead in your sins. I will pray to God that after you have killed me, He will spare you from eternal destruction."

The tall one took a step towards me and then stopped. In an instant, his face was changed. His hatred had turned to curiosity. He lowered his gun and motioned to the others to do the same. They stared at him in amazement, but they took their guns from my face.

Then the tall one spoke again. "Will you pray for us now?" he asked.

I thought my ears were playing a trick. I looked at him and then at the others. My mind was completely paralyzed …

"Father in heaven," I prayed, "you who have forgiven men in the past, forgive these men also. Do not let them perish in their sins but bring them into yourself."

It was a simple prayer, prayed in deep fear. But God looked beyond my fears and when I lifted my head, the men standing in front of me were not the same men who had followed me into the vestry. Something had changed in their faces.

It was the tall one who spoke first. His voice was bold but there was no contempt in his words, "You have helped us," he said, "and we will help you. We will speak to the rest of our company, and they will leave you alone. Do not fear for your life. It is in our hands, and you will be protected."

I was too astonished to reply. The tall one only motioned for the others to leave. He himself stepped to the doorway and then he turned to speak one last time. "I saw widows and orphans in your congregation," he said. "I saw them singing and giving praise. Why are they happy when death is so near?"

It was still difficult to speak but I answered him. "Because they are loved by God. He has given them life, and will give life to those they loved, because they died in Him."

His question seemed strange to me, but he did not stay to explain. He only shook his head in perplexity and walked out the door.

I stared at the open door of the vestry for several moments and then sat down on a nearby straw mat chair. My knees were no longer strong and I could feel my whole body tremble. I could not think clearly. Less than 10 minutes before, I had considered myself a dead man. Even though I was surrounded by 7,000 people there was no human being to whom I could appeal ...

I could not ask the elders to pray, I could not appeal to the mercy of the Nubian killers. My mouth had frozen and I had no clever words to speak. In that moment, with death so near, it was not my sermon that gave me courage, or an idea from Scripture. It was Jesus Christ, the living Lord.[45]

In a second book, Pastor Sempangi shares that those five men subsequently became followers of Jesus Christ, and one of them later became his driver and travelling companion.[46] On a ministry trip to Uganda in December, 2017, I learned that elderly Kefa Sempangi was still effectively ministering in his home country and continuing to care for many orphans.

Our brothers and sisters around the world often express the conviction that Jesus Christ did not come to take away our pain and suffering but to share in it. In the midst of great suffering, they have come to understand the depth of love.

In the Foreword to Pastor Sempangi's book, Richard Halverson, who served as the chaplain to the United States Senate for thirteen years, compared the courage, endurance, and faithfulness of persecuted Christians abroad to our "comfortable" Western Christianity. He says, "These frighteningly contemporary events ... warn all believers to beware the delusion of a status-quo, this-worldly life-style. *Comfortable conformity to the world in which we live today may be the most subtle form of Christ denial*" (emphasis mine).[47]

This last sentence is worth some meditating and soul searching!

Twenty-six months after twenty-one Egyptian Coptic Christians were beheaded by ISIS terrorists on a beach in neighboring Libya while reciting the Lord's Prayer, suicide bombers struck against the church in Egypt again. On Palm

Sunday 2017, forty-nine people were killed—some outside St. Mark's Church in Alexandria and others inside St. George's Church in Tanta, Egypt.

On the following night, the Monday Pascha service of Holy Week, Father Boules George spoke to a packed-out church congregation in Cairo. His words were broadcast on the popular Coptic TV station Aghapy. The title of his sermon was "A Message to Those Who Kill Us."[48] English translations of this message are abundant on the Internet. Father George's three-point outline was: 1. We Thank You; 2. We Love You; 3. We Pray for You.

In his first point, "We Thank You," he made three comments. He thanked them because to die for and because of Jesus is the greatest honour a Christian could have. Also, he thanked them because they shortened the journey of these believers as they were already heading for their ultimate home. And he thanked them because they helped fulfill Jesus's prediction that they were sent out as "lambs among wolves." With just their faith and no weapons in their hands, the people who died fulfilled the words of Jesus.

As an adjunct to point number one, Father George thanked them because usually, their church services on Monday night after a long Palm Sunday celebration are not well-attended, and this event brought people to church on Monday Pascha in numbers rarely seen in Egypt.

In his second point, "We Love You," he shared that those who want to kill them would not likely understand this. He took this opportunity to focus on Jesus's teaching about loving others—even your enemies. And he concluded that, as a result of following Jesus's teaching, Christians are to love others no matter what they do to them.

Point three, "We Pray for You," was an opportunity to also teach his own people. "Instead of being upset, are you praying for those who want to kill us?" He mentioned specifically prayer so their persecutors could sleep at night. "Can you imagine? We are being slaughtered and the King of Peace gives us peace to sleep. And the one who slaughters can't sleep all night." He mentioned this was the case with the king during the night when Daniel was in the lion's den. Father Boules George ended this point with the powerful statement, "We must ALL pray for them today that God opens their eyes and opens their hearts to His love. Because if they knew Him, they could NEVER do this."

He closed his message with the words of Jesus in His Olivet Discourse: "So you have sorrow now, but I will see you again; then you will rejoice, and *no one can rob you of that joy*" (John 16:22, emphasis mine).

Naseem Faheem, a guard at St. Mark's Cathedral in Alexandria, was one who died. On Palm Sunday, he had stopped a suicide bomber and redirected him through the perimeter metal detector, where the terrorist's bomb detonated. Likely the first to die in the blast, Faheem saved the lives of dozens inside the church. Later that week, his widow was interviewed on the most prominent TV talk show. She said with her children by her side, "I'm not angry at the one who did this. I'm telling him, 'May God forgive you, and we also forgive you. Believe me, we forgive you. You put my husband in a place I couldn't have dreamed of.'"

As the camera came back to popular host Amr Adeeb, there was twelve seconds of dead air as he searched for words to respond. As a broadcaster myself, twelve seconds of dead air seems like an eternity. Stunned, he finally stammered, "The Copts of Egypt … are made of … steel!" He went on to mutter about Copts bearing atrocities over hundreds of years but couldn't escape the central scandal. "How great is this forgiveness you have!" his voice cracked. "If it were my father, I could never say this. But this is their faith and religious conviction." Millions marvelled with him across the airwaves of Egypt.[49]

When lambs follow "the Jesus way," the wolves at least take notice.

Since 1975, Bengali pastors in Bangladesh have faced increasing persecution for preaching the gospel. Some are beaten, imprisoned, or even killed. As a result, their wives and children often face isolation. They are verbally and physically abused, and they face an extraordinary challenge to remain free from bitterness. In Bangladesh, Pastor Mir wanted to take the gospel to a place that had not heard about Jesus. So, he brought his wife Anjali and their children to a Muslim community that had never seen a Christian. People came to visit them out of curiosity, assuming Christians must look different somehow.

Over the next several years, people began opening their hearts to the message of Jesus. But others in the village put pressure on the Mirs to leave. On New Year's Eve, Anjali heard a loud noise. Someone was shot. A man had been riding his bike to the market when two men caught him, shot him in the mouth, and then used a dagger to stab him eleven times in critical points of his body.

After a long while, Anjali Mir learned that the man who had been attacked was her husband. She longed to go to him at the hospital, but their two small children required her care. She could not leave. She wept, thinking, *My husband is going to die. What am I going to do? How am I going to raise my two boys?*

Miraculously, Pastor Mir survived. After years of extensive medical treatment, he is preaching the gospel again, but his injuries continue to plague him. His wife still worries over her children's safety. She struggles to explain to the boys why their father was attacked.

Pastor and Mrs. Mir are committed to staying in their village for the sake of their new Christian brothers and sisters. Anjali says, "If we leave, then there will be no church and the people who have just put their faith in Jesus, may fall away … Jesus suffered for us, so we should also be willing to suffer for Him."

The real cry of their heart is wanting to be faithful to Jesus to the end (Revelation 14:12). Patient endurance is an oft-repeated theme throughout the New Testament. It seems to be one we don't talk about or preach about much. Yet it is a constant challenge for members of our persecuted family.

Traian Dorz was a gentle man who led a Christian denomination in Romania during the Communist era. He was a talented poet, writer, and song composer. After his conversion at the age of fifteen, he began to publish spiritual songs and poems. During his lifetime, he wrote seventy-four books. Traian lived in a tiny, impoverished house with one room. The furniture consisted of a few simple wooden chairs, a small table, and an iron bedstead. When a co-worker let his eyes wander over the bare walls and the ceiling, Traian said, "Aren't we rich, brother? Gratitude makes us rich. Gratitude for what Jesus has done for us."

Traian knew tragedy. He was imprisoned for eighteen years and often tortured. The secret police also tried to set him up for an "accident." The years in prison weakened him physically. He was constantly ill. "Suffering brings balance in your life," he once explained. "It's good for your heart. It brings you closer to Jesus."

Visiting Traian was not an easy task. His house was often under guard, making it virtually impossible to get in without being noticed. One day, Dr Paul Negrut visited him, and as he entered the simple home, he realized that Traian was bleeding from open wounds. He asked, "What happened?"

Traian replied, "The Securitate just left my home. They came and confiscated my manuscripts. Then they beat me."

Dr Negrut began to complain about the heavy-handed tactics of the secret police, but Traian stopped him, saying, "Brother Paul, it is such a blessing to suffer for Jesus. God didn't bring us together tonight to complain but to praise Him. Let's kneel down and pray."

He knelt and began praying for the secret police. He asked God to bless them and save them. He told God how much he loved them. He said, "God, if they will come back in the next few days, I pray that you will prepare me to minister to them." By this time, Paul Negrut was ashamed. He thought he had been living a very difficult life in Romania for the Lord. And he was already bitter about that.

Traian Dorz then shared with him how the secret police had been coming to his home regularly for several years. They beat him twice every week. They confiscated all his papers. After the beating he would turn to the officer in charge, look into his eyes, and say, "Mister, I love you. And I want you to know that if our next meeting is before the judgement throne of God, you will not go to hell because I hate you but because you rejected love." Traian repeated these words after every beating.

One evening years later, that officer came alone to Traian's home. Traian prepared himself for another beating. But the officer spoke kindly and said, "Mr. Dorz, the next time we meet will be before the judgement throne of God. I came tonight to apologize for what I did to you and to tell you that your love moved my heart. I have asked Christ to save me. Two days ago, the doctor discovered that I have a very severe case of cancer and I have only a few weeks to live before I go to be with God. I came tonight to tell you that we will be together on the other side."

Traian Dorz died in 1989, just before the fall of Ceaușescu, Romania's notorious dictator. His final message to the West was this: "All our prayers and all our love are hastening the coming of our Lord Jesus. Then we will all be at home and we'll speak one language. Until then, we live with the message from Ephesians 6:24, Grace to all who love our Lord Jesus Christ with an undying love."

These stories illustrate wonderful grace in responses to serious opposition. But is there ever a time to cross the line and become positively aggressive?

6
CROSSING THE LINE

The only thing necessary for the triumph of evil is for good men to do nothing.
Edmund Burke

Commitment to Jesus—even to the death—is an honorable and worthy goal of any disciple. But there is always a question posed as to these characteristics and teachings of Jesus we've discussed and will continue to examine. Is there ever a line that we cross when the "wise as snakes and harmless as doves" directive challenges us to change from a reactive posture of total humility, submission, and grace to an aggressive one of boldness, bravery, and bravado?

This question is especially relevant to those of us who live in Western societies based on freedom, justice, and the rule of law. We are not yet subjected to complete totalitarianism as many others are today around our world. So where is the line we cross when we must take a stand for defending our freedoms and opposing tyranny?

I am currently reading a chapter each morning of a very interesting book series titled *The Christians: Their First Two Thousand Years*—an excellent twelve-volume series covering the two millennia of church history since the days of Jesus. The final volume covers the twentieth century and is subtitled *The High Tide and the Turn*. I'm up to the Second World War in my reading, and today's chapter was titled "Some Christians Spoke Out and Died."[50] It outlines a small group of Christian German men who opposed the Hitler regime. One of them was my hero, Dietrich Bonhoeffer, who "ran an underground seminary, used his international connections to aid refugees and accused inactive fellow Christians of relying on 'cheap grace' … he served as a courier connecting the German resistance movement to Allied intelligence."

Bonhoeffer argued that to maintain one's innocence in a setting such as the Third Reich, even to the point of not plotting Hitler's death, would be irresponsible action. To refuse to engage oneself in the demands of *necessita*, would be the selfish act of those who cared for their own innocence, who cared for their own guiltlessness, more than they cared for their guilty brothers and sisters. He called that Satan's temptation to die with clean hands and a dirty heart.[51]

Bonhoeffer, a strong and committed disciple of Jesus Christ, gave us a good example of crossing the line and doing it "with grace." He paid the price for it with his life just weeks before the Allies defeated Germany. Yet he would not consider himself a martyr.

He blamed himself and all German Christians for permitting the Nazi revolution to occur. In 1932, the year before Hitler took power, he foresaw what would happen: "The blood of martyrs might once again be demanded," he said, "but this blood, if we really have the loyalty and courage to shed it, will not be innocent, shining like that of the first witnesses for the faith. On our blood lies heavy guilt, the guilt of the unprofitable servant who is cast into outer darkness."[52]

A medical doctor describes Bonhoeffer in his dying hour:

Through the half-open door of his cell, I saw the pastor kneeling in prayer. I have never been so moved as I was then. His devotion was absolute; he appeared almost cheerful. Later in front of the gallows, he repeated a short prayer, then climbed up to the rope with complete composure. He was dead in a few seconds. During my fifty years' experience in medicine, I have never seen anyone die so calmly and so trustingly.[53]

Corrie ten Boom crossed the line repeatedly in Haarlem, Netherlands, during the Second World War. Hiding Jews in her home was her way of resisting evil. When the Gestapo would come to her home, they'd ask (based on suspicions), "Are you hiding any Jews here in your home…?" She knew they left off the rest of the question: "…that we can arrest and take off to the camps?" She would answer "No! (I don't have any Jews here that you can arrest and drag off to the camps!)." She was responsible for saving many lives.

A significant event followed hard on the heels of the Second World War in Germany that warrants our remembering because it so rarely happens internationally without violence. Following the war, the Allies divided defeated Germany into four zones supervised by the countries of USA, England, France, and the Soviet Union. The Soviets had agreed to give up two thirds of the city of Berlin to the French, British, and Americans as it lay inside the Soviet zone. Obviously, the Soviets were given the eastern section, which meant that West Berlin was a capitalist island in the middle of a Communist state.

Postwar aid to implement the restoration of free Western Europe was provided by the USA in their Marshall Plan involving billions of dollars. The only vulnerable weak point where the Soviets—not wanting an economically prosperous western Europe—could strike back was blockading the three western sections of the city of Berlin. The first announcement was made on New Year's Day in 1948, and a total blockade began June 1, 1948. This meant stopping rail transportation, road traffic, and water access. The people of West Berlin were essentially under siege.

The Allied countries were tired of war and unwilling to return to its horrendous violence. But they were also not willing to acquiesce. President Truman of the USA declared his country would stay in West Berlin and Britain agreed. To accomplish this without warfare required a massive airlift. More than two thousand tons of food would be needed daily as well as 1,200 tons of coal for heating. The airlift itself would consume three hundred thousand barrels of aviation fuel per month after it began in August 1948. All told, more than seventy thousand people, military and civilian, would be involved.

Despite this massive undertaking, by the winter of 1948/49 there were alarming shortfalls of needed supplies. Adjustments were made, and the airlift ultimately worked. Stalin called off the blockade in May 1949, and on August 26 that year, the last British plane landed with needed supplies. On the fuselage of that plane was painted a verse from Psalm 21: "for they intended evil against thee; they imagined a mischievous device, which they were not able to perform." This was one of the twentieth century's greatest examples of not accepting evil yet responding with non-violence. A creative alternative was devised, and it worked.[54]

We in North America currently live in free democratic countries, but this may soon be a challenge for us, as it was for Bonhoeffer in Germany. American

Christian author Rod Dreher has written a new book of warning to us all, titled *Live Not by Lies: A Manual for Christian Dissidents*. His research was prompted by repeated alarms from immigrants to the USA from Eastern Europe and the old Soviet Union. They see our societies drifting toward what they call "soft totalitarianism." Their foundational belief is that all totalitarian regimes are based on lies. Hence the title of Dreher's book, based on the 1974 essay by Aleksandr Solzhenitsyn.

Dreher went to Russia and Eastern Europe to interview many of the dissidents who resisted the Communist regime of their country. Their stories are powerful—especially the Christians who struggled with crossing the line in following Jesus. One of his interviews was with my good friend in Moscow, Alexander Ogorodnikov. I've been a friend of Sasha for more than thirty years following his eight long, difficult years in the Siberian Gulag. He had become a committed Orthodox Christian while in university and began a Bible study movement in Moscow called the Christian Seminar, focusing on other young people, much to the disapproval of the KGB.

Sasha told Rod Dreher,

At one of his seminars there appeared an elderly writer who sat listening to the young Christians—every single one of them had been atheists from good Soviet families—talking about the faith. The visitor said not a word. Finally, he stood up and said that he was the son of a high official of the tsar. He said, "Brothers, you have no idea [of the importance of] what you are doing. If just ten of you had been in Saint Petersburg in 1917, the Revolution would not have happened."[55]

It reminds me of the old adage, "The only thing necessary for evil to triumph is for good people to do nothing!" Today Sasha Ogorodnikov runs a ministry for street people in Moscow. He continues to confront bureaucratic frustrations but has learned to do it with grace.

Dreher also tells the story about Father Kolaković in Czechoslovakia during the early Cold War years after the fall of the Nazis. He taught young Czech and Slovak believers that every person must be accountable to God for his or her actions and that freedom provides the responsibility to live within the truth. He established cell groups of young believers for prayer, study, and fellowship. He called this fast-growing body his "Family."

He said to them "Give yourself totally to Christ, throw all your worries and desires on him, for he has a wide back and you will witness miracles."[56] The essence of his training and teaching turned into a motto: See. Judge. Act.

See: Be awake to realities around you.

Judge: Discern the meaning of these realities based on the truth you know from your Christian faith.

Act: Resist evil based on your conclusions.

In 1946, Czech authorities deported the activist priest. Two years later, communists seized total power, just as Father Kolaković had predicted. Within several years, almost all of the Family had been imprisoned and the Czechoslovak institutional church brutalized into submission. But when the Family members emerged from prison in the 1960s, they began to do as their spiritual father had taught them. [They] quietly set up Christian circles around the country and began to build the underground church. [It] became the principle [*sic*] means of anti-communist dissent for the next forty years.[57]

Several years ago, a young Slovak Christian named Timo Križka set out to honour his ancestor's sacrifice by documenting the suffering and radiating peace in the lives of these now elderly believers. He searched for a message for you and me and others of the "free" world.

The message he found was this: The secular liberal idea of freedom so popular in the West, and among many in his post-communist genera-tion, is a lie. That is, the concept that real freedom is found by liberating the self from all binding commitments (to God, to marriage, to family), and by increasing worldly comforts—that is a road that leads to hell. Križka observed that the only force in society standing in the middle of that wide road yelling "Stop!" were the traditional Christian churches.[58]

The significance is that all of us need to act!—but act on the truth with the grace of our Lord. After sharing the stories of many others who crossed the line, Dreher concludes,

When we act—either to embrace suffering on our own or to share in the sufferings of others—we have to let it change us, as it changed these confessors of the communist yoke. It could make us bitter, angry, and vengeful, or it could serve as a refiner's fire, as it did with Solzhenitsyn

[and] Ogorodnikov, and so many others, purifying our love of God and tortured humanity.[59]

Os Guinness points out this type of commitment:

Are we [in the West] showing that we too are prepared to follow Jesus and his authority at any cost? ... When a mere whiff of incense would have saved their lives, early Christians refused to acknowledge Caesar as lord rather than Jesus and were made human torches or the evening meal for wild animals ...

It is time, and past time, to turn this situation around and take a stand worthy of our Lord—before the cock crows and we are left with the bitter regret that our brothers and sisters around the world stood firm and paid with their lives, but our generation in the West betrayed our Lord in such a pitiful way.[60]

I believe the example of the early church and the teaching of the apostles will help us better understand the dynamics of the countercultural way of living out Jesus's teachings and finding the needed balance between grace and truth.

7

THE EARLY CHURCH

The kingdom ... goes out into the world vulnerable,
suffering, praising, praying, misunderstood, misjudged,
vindicated, celebrating: ... always bearing in the body the
dying of Jesus so that the life of Jesus may also be displayed.

N. T. Wright

The Book of Acts paints the picture of the apostles living out Jesus's imagery of lambs among wolves. From the conversion of three thousand people on the day of Pentecost onward, they faced constant opposition from authorities and others.

As we share in our *Standing Strong Through the Storm* (SSTS) seminars, the early church understood that "weakness" and "persecution" was always the platform for sharing the gospel. It never depended on freedom, approval, or sanction. Theirs was a faith of "strength in weakness" and "wisdom in foolishness" as taught by the apostle Paul. And because earth wasn't their home, they could agree that "living means living for Christ, and dying is even better" (Philippians 1:21).

The New Testament church continued to grow because they modelled the character of Jesus and the power of His Holy Spirit. Their ministry and life objective were given directly to them as Jesus's last words before His ascension: "You will receive power when the Holy Spirit comes upon you. And you will be my witnesses, telling people about me everywhere—in Jerusalem, throughout Judea, in Samaria, and to the ends of the earth" (Acts 1:8).

FEARLESS MARTYRDOM
Bible scholars have long labored over this passage. How would the apostles witness? They would attest and exemplify the "grace and truth" lifestyle of Jesus.

But the word translated "witness" here in the original language is the word for "martyr." A witness also had to be ready to become a martyr, a witness with blood. To be a witness meant to be loyal no matter what the cost.

Jesus had told His disciples on the night before His crucifixion, "Do you remember what I told you? 'A slave is not greater than the master.' Since they persecuted me, naturally they will persecute you. And if they had listened to me, they would listen to you" (John 15:20).

History and church tradition tell us what actually and ultimately happened to each of Jesus's disciples:

- Philip was scourged and crucified.
- Matthew was nailed to the ground with spikes and beheaded.
- Jude was beaten to death with sticks and clubs.
- Simon was tortured and crucified.
- John, the son of Zebedee, was tortured and exiled on Patmos.
- James, the brother of John, was beheaded.
- James (the less) was pushed from the top of a building; then his broken body was beaten to death.
- Andrew, Peter's brother, hung on a cross for three days before dying.
- Bartholomew was beaten and skinned alive before being beheaded.
- Thomas was speared with a javelin.
- Peter was crucified—upside down.

Every single one of our Lord's disciples suffered cruel torture, not for saying Jesus was crucified but for saying He had risen from the dead! The disciples were tortured, vilified, exiled, and executed for their conviction that Jesus Christ is alive, and He is Lord! Yet they accomplished in obedience Jesus's instructions for establishing His church among the nations of the world.

THE CROSS-CENTERED MESSAGE REQUIRES CROSS-BEARING MESSENGERS!

They were courageous and bold because they had lost their fear of dying. Jesus had died for them, risen from the dead, and promised them a place with Him forever. They were thus willing to give everything—even their lives—for Him. To me, this is perhaps the greatest evidence of the reality of Jesus's resurrection. No one is willing to die for a lie, a sham, or a cover-up, certainly not an entire group of people without an exception. The apostles were so convinced of Jesus's literal resurrection that they testified about it in the face of all kinds of opposition and without retaliating in anger or the like—kind even to their premature deaths.

The apostle Paul also often referred to the issue of martyrdom—especially in the letter to the Philippians. Ernst Lohmeyer was a German theologian, a contemporary of Dietrich Bonhoeffer. Lohmeyer was murdered in 1946 by Soviet military operatives. His biographer, James R. Edward, writes:

The structure and content of Philippians, maintained Lohmeyer, were determined by martyrdom: comfort in martyrdom, dangers attending martyrdom, and admonitions in the face of martyrdom.

Lohmeyer regarded Philippians 3:10 as a capsule of the entire epistle, as well as the claim of the gospel on church and believer: "That I may know Jesus Christ and the power of his resurrection, and may share his sufferings, becoming like him in his death."

Martyrdom was the irreducible kernel of Christianity because it was the essential link between the gospel and the world. In martyrdom, the Christian individual and the church collectively testify to the essence of the gospel with a purity and totality that they nowhere else render for the gospel. And also in martyrdom, the world witnesses and experiences the truth and power of the gospel in a way and to a degree that it nowhere else witnesses and experiences the gospel.[61]

COMMUNITY CARE AND DISCIPLESHIP

In Acts 2:42–47, we see a beautiful picture of the thousands of new followers of Jesus living together in meaningful community:

All the believers devoted themselves to the apostles' teaching, and to fellowship, and to sharing in meals (including the Lord's Supper), and to prayer.

A deep sense of awe came over them all, and the apostles performed many miraculous signs and wonders. And all the believers met together in one place and shared everything they had. They sold their property and possessions and shared the money with those in need. They worshiped together at the Temple each day, met in homes for the Lord's Supper, and shared their meals with great joy and generosity—all the while praising God and enjoying the goodwill of all the people. And each day the Lord added to their fellowship those who were being saved.

The living conditions and handling of money may not be prescriptive for all times and eras, but certainly indicate a care for all members of the community in a challenging time that was Christ-honoring.

In his 1985 Gold Medallion winning book, *The Church in China: How It Survives and Prospers Under Communism*, my former colleague Carl Lawrence documents how the church in China under Communism followed the Jerusalem church pattern of Acts 2:42–47 and thrived.[62]

PRAYER FOR BOLDNESS—NOT SAFETY

In Acts 4, Peter and John had been imprisoned, and on release, their lives had been threatened if they continued to speak or teach in the name of Jesus. They returned to the church and reported what happened. The church resorted to prayer, and their prayer is recorded in this chapter. The surprise to people of our generation is that they prayed for boldness (with accompanying signs and wonders) rather than praying for God's protection. We know God was pleased with their prayer because the place where they were praying was shaken by the Holy Spirit's presence. The result was they were filled with the Holy Spirit and spoke God's Word boldly.

THE CONTRAST OF GOD'S PROVIDENCE

In Acts 12, we read that King Herod Agrippa pleased his people by persecuting the church. He had James, the brother of John, executed by the sword. This emboldened the king to also have Peter arrested. Because it was Passover, Peter was not immediately executed but imprisoned under heavy guard for a later public trial. The church went to prayer. I'm sure they had prayed for James too. And perhaps that is why they were so surprised at Peter's miraculous release. God obviously desired Peter's life to be longer to fulfill His purposes. We respect and yield to the Providence of an eternal and holy God. He alone sees the end from the beginning.

METAMORPHOSIS—A RENEWED MIND

Although the apostle Paul ultimately also gave his life as a martyr, his teaching focus was on living the balanced life with grace and truth. One of his most powerful images was written in his letter to the Romans. In Romans 12, he urged believers to give their bodies as a living sacrifice to God as an act of worship, which demands a radical change. He added, "Do not conform to the pattern of this world, but be transformed by the renewing of your mind. Then you will be able to test and approve what God's will is—his good, pleasing and perfect will" (Romans 12:2 NIV).

The J.B. Phillips paraphrase expresses it this way, "*Don't let the world around you squeeze you into its own mould*, but let God re-mould your minds from within, so that you may prove in practice that the plan of God for you is good, meets all his demands and moves towards the goal of true maturity" (emphasis mine).

The apostle Paul talked about transformation using the term "metamorphosis"—changed from the inside out like a butterfly. This same word was used for Jesus's transfiguration, and Paul used it a second time in 2 Corinthians 3:18 to describe our transformation into the likeness of Jesus. An inward change has to happen so that now we live, not a self-centred, but a Christ-centred life. A Christ-renewed mind is in us.

Without exception, whenever Jesus preached, He challenged His followers to reposition themselves and engage with the world from a redemptive and Kingdom perspective: not protecting their faith but proclaiming their faith. Not seeing themselves as victims but engaging as victors. Not fighting to be acknowledged but denying the self and living to die ... Have you ever wondered what the first words were that Jesus preached? Scripture actually tells us this in Matthew 4:17: "From that time on Jesus began to preach, 'Repent, for the kingdom of heaven has come near.'" ...

Jesus clearly believed in transformation and a change of priorities. *Jesus understood the reality that we do not think differently because our lives are renewed; we live differently because our minds are renewed.* The flow of behavioural changes starts with our thoughts. Thoughts lead to actions, actions lead to habits, habits lead to discipline, discipline builds character and character determines destiny ...

We need the mind of Joshua and Caleb who were the only two Israelites in a whole generation who saw the promised land—simply because they "had a different spirit" (Numbers 14:24).[63]

There are too many issues and obstacles in one's mind that need to be addressed for the renewing process to be a once-off event. As we walk our paths in a personal relationship with Christ, He continuously stimulates new growth and transforms our minds into that which is needed for the task or season at hand. But the key that leads to that growth and transformation is found in the very next verse of Romans 12, which is very seldom quoted together with verse 2. "Because of the privilege and authority God has given me, I give each of you this warning: Don't think you are better than you really are. Be honest in your evaluation of yourselves, measuring yourselves by the faith God has given us" (Romans 12:3).

As long as we walk humbly before the Lord our God and acknowledge that we will always be in need of His Spirit for guidance, growth, and the continuous renewing of our minds, He will continue to graciously equip and transform us for the task at hand.[64]

Paul wrote in 2 Corinthians 10:5, "We capture their rebellious thoughts and teach them to obey Christ." The writer of Hebrews suggested we do this by "fixing our thoughts on Jesus" (Hebrews 3:1 NIV), as well as "fixing our eyes on Jesus" (Hebrews 12:2 NIV).

In 1925, Kate B. Wilkinson wrote the following meaningful lyrics which were set to music later that year. One of my favorite hymns:

May the mind of Christ my Savior
Live in me from day to day,
By His love and pow'r controlling
All I do and say.
May the Word of Christ dwell richly
In my heart from hour to hour,
So that all may see I triumph
Only through His pow'r.
May the peace of Christ my Savior
Rule my life in everything,
That I may be calm to comfort
Sick and sorrowing.
May the love of Jesus fill me,
As the waters fill the sea;
Him exalting, self-abasing,
This is victory.

May I run the race before me,

Strong and brave to face the foe,

Looking only unto Jesus

As I onward go. (Public domain.)

THE APOSTLE PAUL'S ADVICE

In almost every one of his letters, the apostle Paul expressed Christian life characteristics that can help us know how to live victoriously in any situation. Here are some examples with highlights (please take the time to read and meditate on these passages):

LOVE IN ACTION

1. In Romans 12:9–21, Paul began with love, joy, patience, humility, hospitality, harmony peace. He ended with not taking revenge and overcoming evil with good.

Don't just pretend to love others. Really love them. Hate what is wrong. Hold tightly to what is good. Love each other with genuine affection, and take delight in honoring each other. Never be lazy, but work hard and serve the Lord enthusiastically. Rejoice in our confident hope. Be patient in trouble, and keep on praying. When God's people are in need, be ready to help them. Always be eager to practice hospitality.

Bless those who persecute you. Don't curse them; pray that God will bless them. Be happy with those who are happy, and weep with those who weep. Live in harmony with each other. Don't be too proud to enjoy the company of ordinary people. And don't think you know it all!

Never pay back evil with more evil. Do things in such a way that everyone can see you are honorable. Do all that you can to live in peace with everyone.

Dear friends, never take revenge. Leave that to the righteous anger of God. For the Scriptures say,

"I will take revenge;

I will pay them back,"

says the LORD.

Instead,

> "If your enemies are hungry, feed them.
>
> If they are thirsty, give them something to drink.
>
> In doing this, you will heap
>
> burning coals of shame on their heads."

Don't let evil conquer you, but conquer evil by doing good.

2. First Corinthians 13:4–8. Paul's well-known discourse on love and its many nuances:

> Love is patient and kind. Love is not jealous or boastful or proud or rude. It does not demand its own way. It is not irritable, and it keeps no record of being wronged. It does not rejoice about injustice but rejoices whenever the truth wins out. Love never gives up, never loses faith, is always hopeful, and endures through every circumstance.
>
> Prophecy and speaking in unknown languages and special knowledge will become useless. But love will last forever!

Notice, the descriptives of love are all action verbs. Popular culture would have you believe that love is primarily a feeling. The apostle Paul taught that love is a verb, love is an action. *Love is a choice.*

3. Galatians 5:22–26 and 6:10. Paul outlined the fruit of the Holy Spirit and ended with instruction to do good to all people.

> The Holy Spirit produces this kind of fruit in our lives: love, joy, peace, patience, kindness, goodness, faithfulness, gentleness, and self-control. There is no law against these things!
>
> Those who belong to Christ Jesus have nailed the passions and desires of their sinful nature to his cross and crucified them there. Since we are living by the Spirit, let us follow the Spirit's leading in every part of our lives. Let us not become conceited, or provoke one another, or be jealous of one another.
>
> Therefore, whenever we have the opportunity, we should do good to everyone—especially to those in the family of faith.

4. In Ephesians 4:25–32, Paul began with how to live truthfully and ended with kindness, compassion and forgiveness. In Philippians 2:1–11, he began with challenges for humility, love, and concern for others and ended with a poem on having the same servant attitude as Christ. In Colossians

3:1–15, Paul outlined his rules for holy living, and in 1 Thessalonians 4:1–8, he described the controlled lifestyle that pleases God, concluding with "God has called us to live holy lives, not impure lives. Therefore, anyone who refuses to live by these rules is not disobeying human teaching but is rejecting God, who gives his Holy Spirit to you."

THE APOSTLE PETER'S ADVICE

Peter wrote his first letter to first-century churches and believers, who were experiencing significant pressures because of their newfound faith. He told them to not be surprised at their painful trials but rejoice that they were participating in Christ's sufferings. Peter added that we should not be ashamed when we suffer for being a Christian:

Dear friends, don't be surprised at the fiery trials you are going through, as if something strange were happening to you. Instead, be very glad— for these trials make you partners with Christ in his suffering, so that you will have the wonderful joy of seeing his glory when it is revealed to all the world.

If you are insulted because you bear the name of Christ, you will be blessed, for the glorious Spirit of God rests upon you … It is no shame to suffer for being a Christian. Praise God for the privilege of being called by his name! (1 Peter 4:12–14, 16)

I encourage you to read through Peter's short first letter from the perspective of finding encouragement when suffering for Christ.

Peter began his second letter with a crescendo of virtues, the greatest and pinnacle being love. In 2 Peter 1:5–9 he said,

In view of all this, make every effort to respond to God's promises. Supplement your faith with a generous provision of moral excellence, and moral excellence with knowledge, and knowledge with self-control, and self-control with patient endurance, and patient endurance with godliness, and godliness with brotherly affection, and brotherly affection with love for everyone.

The more you grow like this, the more productive and useful you will be in your knowledge of our Lord Jesus Christ. But those who fail to develop in this way are shortsighted or blind, forgetting that they have been cleansed from their old sins.

In the last chapter of his letter, Peter talked about the return of the Lord and the destruction of everything for the recreation of a new heaven and a new earth where righteousness dwells. He then made a powerful statement about how we should live considering this. "Since everything around us is going to be destroyed like this, *what holy and godly lives* you should live, looking forward to the day of God and hurrying it along" (2 Peter 3:11–12, emphasis mine).

RESPOND AS CHRIST RESPONDED

Peter also taught that when we suffer, we should respond as Christ responded. We are to follow His example (see 1 Peter 2:21–25). Jesus did not return insult for insult. He did not threaten. He did not ask for revenge on those who wronged Him. He loved them and prayed for them. We are told to bless those who curse us, love those who hate us, and pray for those who persecute us (Matthew 5:38–48). If we respond in the flesh when we suffer, our suffering may lose its value as a witness to a lost world of wolves. Overseas Christians often report that leaders of persecution against them became believers—because of *how* Christians took the abuse (see 1 Peter 3:8–17).

Aunty Esther Li was the first English-speaking Christian I met in China forty years ago. She was a diminutive elderly Chinese medical doctor with a soft, kind voice that masked the many years of suffering through which she had passed.

"During the Cultural Revolution," she said, "I was called in by my superior one day. At that time, I was in charge of eight large pediatric wards in my hospital.

"The Communists were cracking down on people who did not toe the current party line. My superior warned me that I should deny my publicly declared faith and join the Communist Party, or I may have to face the serious consequences of job demotion and salary reduction.

"A few days later, I was rudely awakened by four nurses who roughly pulled me from my bed and marched me to the hospital. En route, they stopped at a barbershop and shaved off half of my hair. In front of the rest of the staff, I was confronted to renounce my faith in Christ and join the Communist Party.

"I responded, 'I can't deny Jesus. I love Jesus!' At the mention of His name, they threw me down on the ground and cursed. Later, the Communist cadre at my hospital tore the stethoscope from my neck and said, 'You are no longer Esther; you are now The Fool.'"

For the next eleven years, she lived in the basement of the hospital and obediently submitted to her new task—cleaning the floors and toilets of the hospital wards that she previously headed. Her already meagre salary of fifty dollars per month was reduced to fifteen dollars. And she had to buy the cleaning materials from it. The rest was used up on food.

But Esther practised the presence of Jesus in her job. She sang as she toiled. With a twinkle in her eyes she added, "My hospital had the cleanest floors and cleanest toilets in all of China!"

Hospital staff would come to her and with great envy question her source of joy in spite of her troubles. Esther responded, "When you have Jesus in your heart, it doesn't matter what job you do or what position you have. It only matters that you love Him and are faithful and loyal to Him!"

When the Cultural Revolution period ended, Aunty Esther was reinstated in her original job and given all the back pay of which she had been deprived during those eleven years. This amount enabled her to send her daughter to higher education. She faithfully carried on her public witness for Jesus until the day she died in her late nineties.

Jesus also said in Luke 6:23 that the reason for responding with great rejoicing in your suffering is because the persecuted disciple of Jesus is going to receive a great reward in heaven and is in the company of the prophets of old who also received this kind of treatment. Can we realistically "leap for joy" in the face of persecution?

Pastor Richard Wurmbrand was languishing in a Romanian prison cell after months of torture and isolation.[65] He was meditating on this Scripture (Luke 6:23) and decided to make a literal application. So Richard danced—as much as anyone could dance in a cell three paces square—leaping about the room like a madman. The first time he did it, the guard really did think he had gone mad. It was one of the guard's duties to watch for signs that a prisoner's mind was beginning to crack under the strain of imprisonment, for, if he went to pieces, a prisoner would be of no more use for questioning.

So the guard rushed off to his canteen and came back with a hunk of bread and some cheese and sugar and broke the rule of silence as he tried to soothe this strange, laughing, capering figure. Richard ate the food gratefully. It was a very large hunk of bread, far more than he usually had in a whole week!

PAUL ESTABROOKS

Richard Wurmbrand shared how encouraged he was at responding literally to Jesus's direction to react to persecution with great joy and rejoicing! He had received a reward on earth as well as in heaven. Today, the ministry he founded, Voice of the Martyrs, continues his great work among persecuted Christians.

8
REALITIES OF LIVING AS EXILES IN BABYLON

*It's not the Christianity of Constantine
that can face the challenge of secularism,
but the Christianity of the catacombs.*

Brian Zahnd

The Babylonian empire was the most powerful state in the ancient world after the fall of the Assyrian empire (612 BC). Its large, solidly built capital city, Babylon, was beautifully bejewelled by King Nebuchadnezzar, who erected several famous buildings and gardens. It was known as a city devoted to materialism and sensual pleasure. The name Babylon occurs approximately two hundred times in Scripture. Biblical writers used the city to represent paganism and idolatry. We read about it in Jeremiah and in Daniel from the perspective of an exile. Babylon is characterized as a culture set against the purposes of God.

The empire fell more than five centuries before Jesus lived on earth, but its spirit survived in later empires—most notably Rome. During the era of Rome's persecution of Christians, writers of Scripture used the name Babylon as a semi-veiled reference to Rome. There is also the rise and fall of a future Babylon in Revelation 18.

In our days, a significant number of recent Christian books have the name Babylon in the title (see Appendix C – Recommended Reading). Erwin Lutzer, in his perceptive volume *The Church in Babylon*, says the Babylonian culture was characterized by idolatry, immorality, and violence. He sees Christians today as much like Daniel and the other exiles—not geographically but morally and spiritually. And like Israel in Babylon, our challenge is to impact the culture without being spiritually destroyed or contaminated by it.[66]

Metaphorically we can truly consider ourselves living in Babylon like Daniel. Our ability to impact the moral and biblical trends of our society is eroding. This does not mean we curl up and quit or stick our heads in the sand, succumbing to what author Gad Saad has insightfully termed "Ostrich Parasitic Syndrome."[67] But we must become more realistic as to what we can expect when facing challenges against us because of our faith—especially when we don't hide our faith and speak up about moral issues.

YOU'RE FIRED!

We saw in chapter 2 how easily Kelvin Cochran lost his job over something that had no direct relationship to his work or his co-workers. There are many more similar situations occurring across the land.

Popular writer Randy Alcorn describes a scene in his book *Safely Home* that is becoming more commonplace than fictional. Doug is called into the boss's office one Monday morning upon arriving at work. We learn that they are cousins, but Ben, the boss, is upset because on this day he has to fire Doug for twelve counts of reported "hate speech" against diversity, equality, and inclusion. Ben says to his cousin, Doug:

"I was raised in a home with beliefs like yours, remember? Your mom and mine, they were into that ... religious stuff. Okay, I can respect that. And frankly, I don't care how narrow or intolerant you are in the privacy of your own home. But why couldn't you put a lid on it in the office? It's been building up for years. Now you've crossed the line. I've tried to warn you. You've become a disruption ...

"Why do you have to be so narrow, Doug? This attitude of 'I'm right and everybody else is going to hell' just doesn't cut it. Legal says it falls under the category of bigotry, and if we just stand by and let you inflict your bigotry on our employees, [the company] can be held liable ... I've gone to bat for you twice, Doug, but no more. People think I'm protecting you because we're related. They wonder if I'm sympathetic to your beliefs."

"Are you?"

"No, frankly, I'm not. But perception is everything ... The bottom line is, the management team met last week. You were on the agenda. I didn't want to do this, but ... you've forced my hand."

Doug and his cousin, Ben, have a long discourse and repartee. One of Doug's rebuttals is this:

"My own sister's a lesbian, and you know I love her. She lived with us when she was suicidal. I'd give my right arm for her. I'm not telling people they can't live that way. But when we're required to be at a diversity seminar and the instructor is insisting there's no such thing as right and wrong, I'm not going to sit there and be quiet. I'll respectfully speak up. That's what I did. I didn't shoot anybody; I just disagreed. It's America, remember?"[68]

Free country or not, Doug has "crossed the line"—even respectfully—and he loses his job.

On his *Breakpoint* daily editorial, January 1, 2019, John Stonestreet was itemizing priorities for the new year ahead. He said, "2019 might be the year Christians ought to get serious about developing that 'theology of getting fired.' That is, it's time for us to decide when losing our jobs and livelihoods for refusing to go along with the new sexual orthodoxy is exactly what Jesus expects of us."[69]

While I have great respect for John (and read his excellent editorials faithfully), I doubt there will ever be such a "theology." That's because losing your job because of your faith or worldview position is part of a greater biblical theological construct, the "Theology of Suffering."

One year after Stonestreet made his statement, Grayson Gilbert wrote a perceptive blog on the *Patheos* website subtitled "When persecution comes from inside the church." He laments our weak theology of suffering:

Out of that weak theology of suffering comes an inability to willingly and joyfully endure our present sufferings for what gets produced as a result. The American gospel has so long imbibed a gospel message devoid of telling people of the cost it takes to follow Christ, and the reason I believe this is so, is that many do not believe it themselves. In many ways, they've yet to see the hardship and suffering Christ says is part and parcel of following Him. Even those of us who see it plainly in

Scripture don't necessarily "get it" because we are more inclined to see the kind of luxury-suffering indicative of a soft generation, as suffering for our faith.

What I mean by this is that we sense it to be suffering when we are passed over for a promotion, we don't have as many friends as we once had, because of our Christian convictions, or we aren't able to find a spouse ... In other words: we confuse the natural results of living as a Christian in the midst of a broken and fallen world with genuine suffering and persecution, but this is not the way the Bible portrays suffering for the sake of the gospel. Rather, these would all be issues the apostle Paul speaks into to challenge our presuppositions and the object of our affections ... people tend to surmise that the only valid form of suffering and persecution for the sake of the gospel is physical persecution. I believe they are guilty of neglecting that there are varying degrees of persecution, which were even present in the life of Christ as He made His way to Golgotha. As a result, they have no accurate categories to see the writing on the wall when it comes to how swiftly we are actually approaching the days when physical persecution is the norm yet again.[70]

Yes, we should probably even expect that we may lose our job or "be fired" if we continue to stand for what we believe is right and true—even when we do it with grace and respect. But we also must remember the other side of the issue. We know nothing can ever separate us from the love of God, and Jesus has promised His presence and peace when we receive opposition because of His life reflected in and through us.

ANGER

The moral changes and political correctness of many wolves can cause deep resentment in Jesus followers, which can boil over in raw anger. So many sheep see modern thinking as not just a moral issue but also illogical and lacking any degree of common sense. Teaching young children that there are multiple genders to which they can aspire rather than the obvious two God-created genders makes many Christian parents downright livid. This concept even goes against the world's so-called rules of "science" they use to explain everything else.

Are we justified in being angry at issues like these? When we look at the Bible, our guidebook, we see that ever since the fall of man, God the Father could become angry. Throughout the Pentateuch, His anger is described in anthropomorphic terms. God gave His law to regulate Israel's affairs as a nation so that God's elect people would be a beacon of His grace to the whole world (Deuteronomy 4:1–8). He told Moses in Exodus 34:6 that He was slow to anger, but Moses also knew that if you disobeyed His law, His anger could be "furious" (Deuteronomy 9:19).

The Psalmist added to the picture by declaring that God's anger lasts only a moment (Psalm 30:5), while His favour lasts a lifetime. The wise man, Solomon, declared that the wise do not "fly off the handle" but control their anger (Proverbs 14:29), and "a hot temper shows great foolishness."

The New Testament shows us pictures of Jesus in moments of anger. When His Father's "House of Prayer" was being desecrated by merchandizing, He angrily drove them out and turned over the moneychangers' tables. They had to scramble after their rolling coins. Almost a comical picture.

Jesus' harshest words weren't reserved for the Romans, who ruthlessly ruled the world of His time. Those austere words were rightfully given to the Pharisees and those who taught the law, who He called a "brood of vipers." To these abusive religious leaders, Jesus said:

"What sorrow awaits you teachers of religious law and you Pharisees. Hypocrites! For you are like whitewashed tombs—beautiful on the outside but filled on the inside with dead people's bones and all sorts of impurity. Outwardly you look like righteous people, but inwardly your hearts are filled with hypocrisy and lawlessness." (Matthew 23:27–28)

When the religious leaders, who were supposed to be leading the people to God and His grace, were doing just the opposite and burdening the people, even more, Jesus had strong words, spoken directly, to denounce them. We call this "righteous anger."

What then is the difference between righteous and unrighteous anger? Though it is often hard to tell the two apart, we do need to distinguish between them. Unrighteous anger is only concerned to protect or promote oneself, whereas righteous anger reflects God's hatred of evil and love of justice (Romans 9:22). The apostle Paul went on to say that even God is patient in showing His anger.

Not everyone is commissioned to speak publicly on God's behalf. Those who are commissioned must also be careful about impatient anger lest they be disqualified like Moses. In Deuteronomy 32:51, God told Moses that he and Aaron, his brother, would not enter the Promised Land with the people because they betrayed God by failing to demonstrate His holiness to the people in the fit of impatient anger when Moses struck the rock by the waters of Meribah at Kadesh.

The apostle Paul brought some balance in Ephesians 4:26–27: "Don't sin by letting anger control you. Don't let the sun go down while you are still angry, for anger gives a foothold to the devil." Verse 26 is a quote from Psalm 4:4 in the Septuagint.[71] Anger must be controlled, resolved quickly, and not allowed to stew, or it will give a foothold to the devil. And then in verses 31–32 of the same chapter, Paul said that God's people are to be gentle and gracious, not harsh or angry.

Many Christians believe in endless grace but want to know if or when there is a proper time for it to be mixed with righteous anger or blunt open opposition. There is so much deceit and treachery in the world these days. Do we just ignore it all? When and how do we speak out?

Based on how we have struggled over this in recent years, I would conclude that each of us must have a clear understanding of the balance needed between grace and truth. Even though there were a few outbreaks of righteous indignation in Jesus's life, His closest disciple declared Him *full* of grace and truth, The leader of His disciples, Peter, declared we must follow in the steps of Jesus, our example, and suffer as He suffered: "He never sinned, nor ever deceived anyone. He did not retaliate when he was insulted, nor threaten revenge when he suffered. He left his case in the hands of God, who always judges fairly" (1 Peter 2:22–23).

In the next chapter, Peter challenged us to always be ready to explain our faith to anyone who asks. Then comes the kicker. Do it in a "gentle" and "respectful" way (1 Peter 3:15–16). I believe God's Spirit has gifted a few spokespersons in the Christian community to publicly call out the deceit and treachery of the culture. We "everyday" Christians need to back up our spokespeople by living a life of love and grace among our daily contacts, including on social media. Lambs do not lash out at people, not even their enemies. Neither can we expect to be treated any differently than Jesus, our Shepherd and Lord, was treated.

Let's allow Jesus' brother, James, to declare the bottom line on this issue. He wrote: "Understand this, my dear brothers and sisters: You must all be quick to listen, slow to speak, and slow to get angry. Human anger does not produce the righteousness God desires" (James 1:19–20).

RESPECT

One of the accusations against us is our lack of respect when responding to our exile in "Babylonian" culture and neighbours. This is most egregiously obvious in social media. Respect is admiration for a person because of his or her position, abilities, qualities, or achievements. Respect is associated with esteem, regard, high opinion, admiration, reverence, deference, and honour. Disrespect is the opposite of respect: it is failing to acknowledge another's worth, withholding the honour that should be given, or actively demeaning someone.

The Bible is not silent when it comes to this issue. Respect is seen more specifically as the act of acknowledging another person's worth, especially because of position, honour, or age. Romans 13:7 says respect should be given to those who are owed respect. There are four categories of people who should be shown respect according to the Bible:

- Elders are owed respect because of their age and experience.
- Authority figures are owed respect, including political leaders, councilmen, church overseers, spiritual leaders, good fathers who discipline their children, parents in general, husbands, wives, and the masters of servants or slaves. Interestingly, slaves are told to respect their masters not only when their masters are good and gentle, but also when they are harsh and unjust.
- Jesus Christ deserves the honour and respect of people, but He was given much disrespect when He came to save. This was especially true in Jesus's home region of Galilee.
- Finally, respect is something owed to all people, simply based on our humanity. We each bear the image of God.

Peter taught that as we witness to the truth and the hope that we have in Christ, we should do it with gentleness and not show disrespect. He summed up the virtue of respect nicely in 1 Peter 2:17: "Respect everyone, and love the family of believers. Fear God, and respect the king."

The "king" of the times was the Roman emperor, Nero, one of the most infamous and corrupt rulers in history. Both the apostles Paul and Peter required believers of their day to show him respect and to pray for him. Nero would ultimately call for the execution of both apostles in Rome in the mid to late 60s.

In a world where people are treated as commodities or as opponents, we followers of Jesus will dignify all people as image bearers of God.

CIVIL DISOBEDIENCE

Even when we control our anger and treat others with respect, there comes a point where as Bible-based Christians we may have to disobey those in civil authority. How we do that with grace distinguishes us from those who are simply rebellious. We see how Daniel and his three friends disobeyed during their time in old Babylon. And God honoured their faithfulness.

I was impressed with a message on YouTube by YWAM teacher, Ms. Landa Cope. Part of her presentation incorporated these words:

We are not the Jews in Israel, we are the believers in Babylon … We don't expect to be in control, we expect to serve. We expect to be light in the midst of the darkness; we are not afraid of darkness. We actually enjoy darkness because we look our best. So literally we don't worry when things get dark because those are the easier times for light to function. We are here to bless the nations, we are here to bless the Babylonians. We have already won our victory; we already have our future in Christ. We are ambassadors of a culture and a lifestyle that is already secured for us forever. We can never be marginalized; we can only believe we are marginalized.[72]

Pastor Wang Yi in China was faced with a challenging decision. He is the founding pastor of Early Rain Covenant Church in Chengdu. In 2005, he was converted, baptized, and started to serve in the house church movement. He was among the few pioneering Christian human-rights attorneys in China. His decision was whether or not to obey the Chinese government about the regulation of church meetings. Pastor Wang felt the government controlled Three Self Church was too nationalistic, creating worship of secular authorities.

On December 9, 2018, he and more than 100 other members of the church were arrested by Chinese authorities, who simultaneously banned any reporting of the crackdown. After he had been detained for forty-eight hours, the Early Rain Covenant Church released Pastor Wang's "My Declaration of Faithful Disobedience" written two months earlier in anticipation of his arrest. Here is an excerpt:

This does not mean that my personal disobedience and the disobedience of the church is in any sense "fighting for rights" or political activism in the form of civil disobedience, because I do not have the intention of changing any institutions or laws of China. As a pastor, the only thing I care about is the disruption of man's sinful nature by this "faithful disobedience" and the testimony it bears for the cross of Christ … *The goal of disobedience is not to change the world but to testify about another world.*[73] (Emphasis mine.)

Pastor Wang repeatedly refers to his position as "faithful disobedience." On December 30, 2019, he was given a prison sentence of nine years by Chengdu Intermediate People's Court for "inciting subversion of state power and illegal business operations." The sentence also included the stripping of his political rights for three years and the confiscation of his personal assets.

Civil disobedience is a complicated topic and worthy of much more coverage than this brief perspective. But for the purpose of our thesis, I make these conclusions:

- Freedom in Christ should not be used to judge others.
- Do not demonize others—even in the name of truth.
- Civil disobedience is to be offered in a spirit of faithfulness.
- Opposition does not define truth—Jesus does.
- A "victim mentality" is un-Christlike.

Now let's look at how some believers define and describe authentic Christianity.

9

FEAR, HATE, AND HARM

The simple fact is that the world will never have any use for Christianity, unless it can prove that it produces the best men and women. The authentic mark of a Christian is a life lived on the standards of Jesus Christ.

William Barclay

More than a decade ago, I was leading one of many annual local church mission trips to the island of Cuba. Before heading to our sister church in the south coast city of Trinidad, we visited the Baptist seminary in Havana, the capital. We were hosted by then-President Dr Leoncio Vegilla, who by this time was elderly and soon to retire and join his son in Florida. He was trained as a medical doctor but became a full-time pastor early in his career. In the difficult decade of the 1960s, he spent five years in prison just because he was a pastor. By the time of our meeting, he had ministered for almost fifty years under the squeeze of Fidel Castro's regime's pressure against the church.

He sat in his favourite chair, giving us a briefing on the history of the school and the church in Cuba. With his signature warm smile, he summarized his conclusion this way: "In all the many years of Christian ministry on this island, we have learned three things: not to fear, not to hate, and not to harm."

He stated these three points in the negative, but each has its positive parallels:

1. Not to **fear** implies boldness and courage.
2. Not to **hate** implies love, forgiveness, and grace.
3. Not to **harm** implies non-violence and aggressive love.

NOT TO FEAR: BOLDNESS AND COURAGE

Fear is a natural human emotion. We especially fear the unknown, change, being injured, and death. Yet there is nothing our adversary would like more than to see us paralyzed with fear—just like King Saul when he faced the Philistines and Goliath (see 1 Samuel 17).

The only fear the Bible condones is "the fear of the LORD" (Proverbs 1:7). The writer of Proverbs makes 14 references to the "fear of the LORD," beginning with Proverbs 1:7 which tells us that "the fear of the LORD is the foundation of true knowledge." To "fear the LORD" means to believe in Him and put your whole soul's commitment on Him. Oswald Chambers made the insightful statement, "The remarkable thing about fearing God is that, when you fear God, you fear nothing else; whereas, if you do not fear God, you fear everything else."

Why do we allow fear to control us? On the one hand, we have past experiences that we don't want to relive, and on the other hand, we are very hesitant about what might lie ahead. But often the events and situations creating the most fear in people have no basis in reality.

All fear is based on perception. Thus, FEAR has been used in the English language as an acronym for "**F**alse **E**vidence **A**ppearing **R**eal." If we could consciously remember this, it would help us to allay many of our fears. That false evidence sometimes is very convincing! However, we must always realize that dread and fear, like other tactics of the enemy, are based on a lie.

This is why throughout the Bible we are repeatedly commanded to "fear not." It is intensely liberating for our witness when we personally overcome the fear of death. This allows us to focus on Christ and His kingdom. The Psalmist said, "I sought the LORD, and he answered me; he delivered me from all my fears" (Psalm 34:4 NIV).

Fear is the serial killer of faith for Christians!

Similar reasons for our personal fears also keep us from being the voice of God in a fallen world on behalf of His church. There is a time for Christians to speak out forcefully against the injustices and sinfulness of our own society and culture. This is especially true in situations where we can help our brothers and sisters who suffer. But fear can keep us tongue-tied. As the church, we must learn to speak out and not be cowed by fear. But do it with grace and respect!

When we are fearful, we can claim the promise of Scripture: "For God has not given us a spirit of fear and timidity, but of power, love and self-discipline" (2 Timothy 1:7). We must always remember who has won the ultimate victory and what Satan's final outcome will be (see Revelation 20:10).

For many in our world today, our number one fear is public speaking. Our number two fear is death. Jerry Seinfeld famously commented, "That means that if you are at a funeral, you are better off in the coffin than giving the eulogy."

We saw earlier that when Jeremiah was still a youth, he was called by the Lord to speak to the spiritual leaders of the nation. It appears he was fearful of the assignment when he said, "I can't speak for you! I'm too young!" But the Lord replied, "Don't be afraid of the people, for I will be with you" (see Jeremiah 1:6–8). One translation has this wording: "Be not *afraid of their faces:* for I am with thee to deliver thee, saith the LORD" (KJV, emphasis added). Looking at the eyes of people while we speak, especially to a group, is for many people an intimidating process. We may wonder whether they like us and agree with our words, or if they are going to turn against us and harm us.

Fear of dying is for most people their number one fear! There is a sense of dread about the unknown ahead. Virtually every fear has a relationship to death and a connection to dying. For example, why are we afraid of flying? The plane may crash, and we may die. That is why Christians around the world take great comfort in the Scripture verses, "Since the children have flesh and blood, he [Jesus] too shared in their humanity so that by his death he might break the power of him who holds the power of death—that is, the devil—and free those who all their lives were held in slavery by their fear of death" (Hebrews 2:14–15 NIV).

At a Standing Strong Through The Storm seminar in Central Asia, our translator looked at us at the close of our three-day session and commented, "Thank you for teaching us how to stand strong. God spoke to me a lot through this seminar. I was afraid to die but not anymore. I have peace to go and spread God's Word." She is now serving the Lord in a strategic mission in her region.

A significant factor in dealing with the fear of dying is realizing that we are *already dead* in Christ (Galatians 2:20). A former colleague, Hector Tamez, says that this concept was clearly seen in the lives of Christians living in war zones of Latin America. The Christians caught in the civil war between the government and Shining Path guerrillas in Peru were a classic example for us. Here is how Hector expressed their commitment:

They know that they are going to be killed. And they say, "In order to be a Christian here, you have to recognize that you are already dead in Christ. Once you recognize this, then any day that passes by in your life is a gain."

In some countries, surviving one day or one year means that you have one God-given day or year to testify not only with your words but with your deeds. Fear should not control your life! Christ should control your life![74]

The Christian must be solidly anchored on seven biblical pillars to combat the fear of dying:

- **God is in control.** He will only allow us to experience what He knows is best for us. We must trust Him as we're encouraged to do in Philippians 4:6–7 and Acts 27:23–25.

- **We are only pilgrims and strangers on this earth.** Our real and final home is heaven. Some of us may be called to enter our heavenly home earlier than we expect. We must be ready (see Hebrews 10:32–39).

- **God can be trusted to ultimately bring good from evil** as we're told in Romans 8:28. Joseph told his brothers, "You intended to harm me, but God intended it all for good" (Genesis 50:20).

- **The enemy can only harm our bodies, not our eternal condition** (Luke 12:4–5). Jesus advised us to get our priorities straight when He said, "Don't be afraid of those who want to kill your body; they cannot touch your soul. Fear only God who can destroy both soul and body in hell" (Matthew 10:28).

- **Focus on fearing God and dying to self.** To "fear" the Lord means to believe in Him and put your whole soul's commitment on Him. "Fear the Lord" is an Old Testament phrase indicating that our trust and belief should be in God rather than fear of others (see also Acts 5:29 and Galatians 2:20).

- **To be absent from the body is to be present with the Lord.** (See 2 Corinthians 5:8 and 2 Timothy 2:11–12.)

- **There is a crown of life for those faithful to death.** (See Revelation 2:10.)[75]

The best summary of this tactic of Satan is written by Nik Ripken in his book, *The Insanity of Obedience.*

Fear is devastating. Fear paralyzes. Fear causes people to run and hide. Fear is a black hole that will deplete joy from the soul of a believer. Fear is a deadly enemy of the church. Your fear is the greatest tool you will ever give to Satan. *Overcoming your fear is your greatest tool against Satan.*[76] (Emphasis mine.)

Maryam and Marziyeh are two former Muslim young ladies from Iran who met in Turkey while being discipled to follow Jesus. They returned together to the capital city of their Muslim motherland to plant new house churches—primarily among young street people. They were successful in this task and, while engaged in this ministry, they would also distribute New Testaments to everyone they met. In the three years of this activity, only once did they meet someone who refused the offer of a New Testament. But they did distribute 20,000 copies. What boldness these young ladies exhibited!

You know that in a country with secret police, activity like this will not last forever. They were ultimately arrested and imprisoned in Iran's notorious Evin prison for 259 days. Most of the pressure on them during interrogations was to return to their former Islamic faith. At first, weakened by hunger and sickness, they struggled with fear. Maryam and Marziyeh were repeatedly interrogated for long periods of time. They were threatened often with statements like, "You must tell us everything about people you have contact with, which organizations you work with. Otherwise, we will lock your hands and feet together and beat you until you die."[77]

The young ladies commented, "Despite our earlier bravado, we were afraid. For all we knew, this could be our last day on earth. We held hands and prayed for strength. *If we are tortured, give us the power to stand fast.*" And God answered their prayers in amazing ways.

After their release, the two young ladies wrote a fascinating biography of their prison experiences titled *Captive in Iran.* They concluded, "For all the heartache we have experienced on this journey, we wouldn't have missed it for anything. It has been our honor to serve Christ in this way, to take up our cross and follow Him faithfully anywhere He leads us."[78]

Working with Open Doors, I loved repeatedly hearing the story of evangelist Gabriel in Colombia from our Latin American co-workers. He sensed a calling of God to take Scriptures (and audio Scriptures for illiterate people) to the opposition guerrilla troops fighting the government military during Colombia's civil war. They moved camps regularly in the mountains of his country. This was extremely risky as many civilians were killed innocently just from the crossfire. Gabriel would load his backpack with gospels and cassettes and head into the mountains. He knew he was near a camp when a posted young guard would step out from behind a large tree and stick a big loaded semi-automatic weapon against his chest.

"Who are you? What are you doing here?" the guard would gruffly demand.

"I'm Gabriel. I've come to share the gospel of Jesus Christ with your troops!"

"We don't want your gospel here. You turn around and get out of here or I will kill you!"

Big guns are usually considered adequate intimidation against anyone you oppose. They are used to create fear. But Gabriel had overcome his fear of death. He would push the barrel of the weapon away from his chest and say, "No you won't! You can't kill me until God says you can kill me."

Most soldiers do not know what to do when their intimidation does not work. Sometimes, it bounces right back at them. Or they are paralyzed with inaction. Gabriel would continue walking right into the camp and begin distributing his Scriptures and start sharing the gospel with those who would listen.

When reporting on his trips, Gabriel would say, "Someday a guarding guerrilla soldier is going to pull the trigger and I will be home with the Lord. But I'm convinced it will not happen until God says so. I have no fear of dying."

My conclusion is this: when we are filled with the Holy Spirit and have lost our fear of death, we are unstoppable until Jesus calls us home to be with Him!

NOT TO HATE: LOVE, FORGIVENESS, AND GRACE

Again, we find a reference to a human emotion that has carried itself to the extreme—to hatred! And in our current society the number of hate crimes is escalating at a serious rate.

The Bible warns about two directions of hatred. One against your brother or countryman (Leviticus 19:17) and the other against ethnic hatred, as is portrayed so clearly in the story of Queen Esther.

The verse in Leviticus recommends confronting people directly and not allowing hatred to develop and control. Throughout the book of Proverbs, Solomon warns more than a dozen times against personal hatred, indicating that living a balanced life will enable the righteous to help and love those who would otherwise cause anger. In the New Testament, Jesus even compares anger or hatred of your "brother" with murder (Matthew 5:22) and reiterates the message, "Love your enemies!" (verse 44).

Selfish pride, a desire to maintain power, and hatred for those who stand in the way have often been the basis for the persecution of racial or religious groups. Many people have died through the centuries because of such hatred. Today also, religious and ethnic hatred can lead to diabolical plans.

Graham and Gladys Staines and their three children were long-term missionaries in India—working mostly among leprosy patients for thirty-four years. On January 22, 1999, fifty-eight-year-old Graham and his two young sons were burned to death when the vehicle they were sleeping in was doused with gasoline and set on fire, allegedly by members of a Hindu fundamentalist group, in the Indian state of Orissa.

Hundreds of millions witnessed widow Gladys Staines forgiving her family's murderers in the name of the gospel on Indian national television—a scene which moved many to tears "and may have achieved more for the gospel in India than many years of missionary work," according to an Indian evangelist.

Describing her prompt forgiveness of the killers as a "spontaneous act," Gladys Staines says, "It took away the bitterness" that otherwise would have remained in her heart. Since the incident she has people coming to her door asking how they can become Christians.

The imagery she used was also powerful. *"Let us burn hatred ... and spread the flame of Christ's love."*

Forgiveness is to be given even when it is not asked for. On the cross, *forgiveness* was one of the first words of Jesus. The soldiers doing the crucifying had not asked for forgiveness, but Jesus realized their need of it.

Forgiveness can only be truly accomplished in the power of the Holy Spirit. But when given, it communicates most powerfully the love of God. And we are called to be like God, to bear God's family resemblance.

Forgiveness is a personal transaction that releases the one offended from the offense. The forgiveness required by the Scriptures is more than detached or limited forgiveness; it is full and complete forgiveness in which there is a total cessation of negative feelings toward the offender and the relationship being restored has the possibility to grow.

On my annual visits to Bethlehem Bible College in Israel's West Bank, I take my tour groups to a hilltop Christian Palestinian encampment called the Tent of Nations nine kilometers southwest of Bethlehem.

I was instructed the first time to do this by an elderly superior. And I am so thankful for his direction. Yet there was no tent or establishment in view, only wilderness, brush, and Israeli settlements on nearby hills as far as the eye could see. We obeyed and began our trek, taking the path less travelled (to borrow from Robert Frost), and that made all the difference. We arrived at an entrance stone that read "WE REFUSE TO BE ENEMIES." We met with Daoud Nassar who shared the history and vision of this Palestinian Christian family's farm project, the Tent of Nations, which was dedicated to the Lord to be a meeting place of reconciliation.

There was a strongly positive attitude in the briefing and sharing. Despite pressures from the nearby surrounding five large Israeli settlements (water and electricity cut off; olive trees destroyed), these Palestinian Christians were determined to reflect no hatred—personal or ethnic—but to share the love of Jesus with everyone they met. It has become a must-visit on any significant Israel tour. I highly recommend it.

Meanwhile, in the East Africa country of Eritrea, for the past twenty years there are so many prisoners who follow Jesus that they are kept in rat- and cockroach-infested metal shipping containers. A young Christian singer without a rebellious bone in her body, Helen Berhane, spent almost three years in the containers because of her faith. She was severely tortured but in spite of that, she had no fear and showed no hatred toward the guards who beat her. Once when interrogated for teaching the Bible to the guards outside her cell, she replied:

> "I am always looking for opportunities to talk about my faith and to spread the news about Jesus. I am not ashamed of the gospel and I will talk to anyone and to everyone. Jesus does not just want me to tell the

prisoners about him, he wants me to tell the guards too. Even if the president were to visit the prison, I would tell him about the gospel.

"I am not afraid of you. You can do what you want to me, but ultimately all you can do is kill my body, you cannot touch my soul. You cannot even kill me unless it is God's will that I should die."[79]

Her persecutors had no answer and returned her to her shipping container.

NOT TO HARM: THE THIRD WAY – NON-VIOLENCE AND AGGRESSIVE LOVE

Uncontrolled hatred can lead to a grudge that can bear violent fruit (1 John 2:10–11, 4:20).

In his books *Engaging the Powers* and *The Powers That Be,* Walter Wink argues that Jesus rejected the two common ways of responding to injustice: violent retaliation and passive acceptance. Instead, Jesus advocated a third way: retaliating with an assertive but non-violent response. He taught "Do not resist an evil person" (Matthew 5:39).

Although we are looking at this principle predominantly from a personal life perspective, it can easily apply nationally and internationally at a government level also. In early 2003, Joe Klein wrote an interesting editorial in *TIME* magazine titled, "Why Not Kill Dictators with Kindness?" He argued that USA's policy (begun by President Woodrow Wilson) of diplomatic ostracism of perceived unjust governments has been an unmitigated disaster, especially with China, lasting almost thirty years and ending in the Vietnam war.

He suggests (which he calls a "wicked thought") doing the one thing that would most discomfort and perhaps even destabilize the precarious regimes of North Korea, Cuba, Iran, Vietnam, Libya, etc. Why not just say, "We hereby grant you diplomatic recognition, whether you like it or not. We're naming an ambassador. We're lifting the embargo. We're going to let our companies sell you all sorts of cool American things like Big Macs and Hummers. This doesn't mean we approve of the way you run your country, but it's silly for us to deny that you're in charge … for now."[80]

Klein quotes an Iranian-American dissident scholar as saying, "There is a theory that American culture and economic power is so insidiously attractive that opening up to the U.S. would be the death of these regimes. I've heard it called the Fatal Hug." And he quotes a foreign policy expert who questions

USA policy of refusing to talk with certain countries perceived to be opponents as asking, "When has it ever helped to refuse to talk? Why voluntarily reduce your influence over an adversary?" My point in sharing this is to indicate that at the governmental level there are multiple perspectives in dealing with perceived enemies that might reduce potential violence.

At a seminar in Indonesia of pastors who had experienced persecution, a former colleague was teaching about our responses to opposition. Most of the group were trained in a pacifist theology. The instructor made a bold announcement. "Brothers and Sisters," he said, "when you are persecuted, you *must* retaliate." A large section of the group stood up shaking their heads, preparing to leave the seminar room and go home.

"Wait a minute," the instructor continued. "You *must* retaliate the Jesus way!" Now he had piqued their curiosity, and they all sat down. "Jesus gives a third way to respond to persecution. You retaliate by *loving* your enemies; *doing good* to those who hate you; *blessing* those who curse you; and *praying* for those who mistreat you." He proceeded to give them a lesson on Luke 6, which we looked at earlier.

As noted in the Introduction, Dr Glen Stassen has long studied Jesus's teachings and calls the third way "transforming initiatives." His books and perspectives are very worthwhile studying.

The key to understanding Stassen's "transforming initiatives" and Wink's "third way" argument is detailed attention to the social customs of the Jewish homeland in the first century and what Jesus's sayings would have meant in that context. We have already seen what it means to "turn the other cheek." That is not all. The teachings about "going the second mile" and "giving your cloak to one who sues you for your coat" make a similar point: they suggest creative non-violent ways of protesting oppression by seeing it as an opportunity.

Christians are thus not people who passively accept ridicule, persecution, and affliction. We retaliate! But we do not retaliate with the weapons or the attitudes of the world. Followers of Christ need to be taught that it is okay to retaliate, but that we need to be filled with the fruit of the Spirit to do so, remembering that even our perceived enemies are also God's image bearers.

If someone hurts us (consider the supreme example set by Christ on the cross), we take revenge by offering love and forgiveness. If someone threatens our safety and security, we take revenge by praying for them. If someone curses us, we bless them. If someone speaks words of hate to us, we retaliate by doing something good to them.

Two things will happen when you show love to your enemy and feed him or give him something to drink: you will heap burning coals on his head, and the Lord will reward you (see Proverbs 25:22).

In the times when Solomon wrote this Proverb (it is also quoted by the apostle Paul in Romans 12), there was a person in every village who tended a fire all night, making hot coals. Early in the morning, this person would load up all the coals into an urn and put it on his head and go from house to house and give each of them enough coals to start their fire. So, heaping coals of fire on his head, means that by feeding your enemy and treating him with kindness, you might make him into a blessing for your community. The Lord who sees and knows all things is the ultimate rewarder.

"Do all that you can to live in peace with everyone" (Romans 12:18).

10

THE DOWNWARD SPIRAL
OF OPPOSITION

*The depravity of man is at once the most
empirically verifiable reality but at the
same time the most intellectually
resisted fact.*

Malcolm Muggeridge

A children's story tells us that a frog accidentally jumped into a pot of hot water on the stove. The frog did not try to jump out of the pot, instead it stayed in it to enjoy the warmth. As the temperature of the water started to rise, the frog managed to adjust its body temperature accordingly. When the water slowly reached the boiling point, the frog then tried to jump out of the pot but was not able to deal with it and boiled to death. So, do you blame the hot water for its death?

The moral of the story is that the frog couldn't make it due to its own inability to perceive the climbing temperature and thus decide when it had to jump out. We all need to adjust according to the situation but there are times when we need to face the situation and take the appropriate action when we have the strength to do so before it's too late to jump out. There are outspoken, trustworthy Christians today who say we are in "hot water" and many of us are like the frog—not aware that the water is heating possibly beyond our ability to withstand it.

Whenever I ask audiences in Western societies to word-associate "persecution," most responses are what are referred to as the "big three": torture, imprisonment, and martyrdom. Many would agree that persecution is much more than the "big three" which are often only experienced as an end result in the stages of persecution. Persecution of a hated segment of society begins gradually and accelerates stage by stage. Christians in the Western world should recognize they are well into the first stages of persecution.

Jesus repeatedly warned His followers that if the world hated Him, it would hate them also (one example is John 15:18). In Luke 6:22, we hear Jesus reminding His disciples that this opposition is a blessing. Not a blessing we ever hear many Christians praying for.

It is thus a very basic awareness that as a follower of Jesus, you can expect opposition, just as Jesus Himself experienced it. "Think of all the hostility he [Jesus] endured from sinful people; then you won't become weary and give up " (Hebrews 12:3). He indicated that opposition would come from the world and possibly even from your own family and friends.

History shows us that this downward spiral of opposition from the world has elements and processes. Do we thus exhibit a persecution complex, a chip on our shoulder attitude? Absolutely not! Nor do we want to be surprised like the frog in the heated water. The good news is that Jesus says we can live a life of joy during these troubles because He has overcome the world and so can we (John 16:33). Keep in mind that Jesus said we are "blessed" when this opposition comes because of Him.

STAGE 1: DISINFORMATION

"God blesses you when people … say all sorts of evil things against you because you are my followers" (Matthew 5:11).

This first element of opposition is characterized by unchecked ridicule and disinformation against a targeted group (Christian or others). In this stage, Christians are robbed of their good reputation and the right to answer the accusations made against them. Media, politics, entertainment, publications, and the academy are most often the avenues used to spread such insinuations or lies.

If disinformation about any group is disseminated long enough, few will defend Christians in later stages because of this negative brainwashing. It essentially dehumanizes the person or group and is a pattern of thinking that may make it easier for milder wrongs to ignite a chain reaction of events. It creates an us-versus-them mentality.

A classic historic example is the gross disinformation the German Nazis spread about the Jews that then developed into a literal negative symbol when Jewish homes and businesses were marked with Stars of David and targeted. This can also result in verbal stereotyping. In the Rwanda genocide, the term *cockroach* became a negative classification of all Tutsis as conspirators against the government.

There are many significant global examples of disinformation used against Christian brothers and sisters. The influence and impact of negative media against Christians in an autonomous region in Central Asia is very strong. A local pastor was shown on TV and, without reference to any evidence, labelled "an enemy of the state." His family members' pictures were also shown at the same time, causing them to be despised by their community. A Christian woman who was shown on TV was not able to continue her work in a kiosk in the market. Other vendors forced her to leave the bazaar. One local pastor said, "Since the program is shown regularly on TV, persecution has become worse. Some people have left the church out of fear. When you start to preach (to the public), people close up and say, we have heard about you, we don't want to listen."

In North Korea, the entire society is controlled by propaganda and disinformation. Persecution is so severe that in many Christian families, children are not even told about the family's faith in Jesus until they are young adults because they are encouraged and expected to inform on their parents while in their school years. Christians are considered enemies of the state and the disinformation about this is widespread.

Similarly, in countries like Laos and Vietnam, the government disinformation is that Christianity is an American religion being used to infiltrate their country rather than the former military methods. All Christians are thus portrayed as being traitors and working for America and the CIA.

STAGE 2: INJUSTICE (DISCRIMINATION)
"He was humiliated and received no justice" (Acts 8:33).

Christians experiencing opposition are following in the footsteps of their master, Jesus. In Acts 8, Philip revealed to the Ethiopian eunuch that the passage from Isaiah 53 he was reading referred to Jesus, who indeed was deprived of justice. Today in the Western world, we would describe His trial before crucifixion as occurring in a "kangaroo court"!

Disinformation defaming any group, including Christians, insulates them from public protection if the group is later victimized by discrimination. Discrimination relegates the group to second-class citizenship with inferior legal, social, political, and economic status. Once discrimination takes place, few will intervene when the mistreatment comes.

Examples of such injustice against Christians abound around the world: ID cards in a country where Christianity is an unacceptable entry in the religion column; daughters abducted because they are Christians; expulsion from the community just because they are committed followers of Jesus.

Christians in Pakistan are a small minority among a large Muslim majority and often face such discrimination. The problem is compounded by the fact that many Christians are illiterate and poor. One teacher at a training center for Christian women recently said, "We do face discrimination because we live in the midst of people who don't want us to move forward; people who keep trying to push us down so that we will always be in slavery."

But one type of injustice against Christians that repeatedly occurs in Pakistan brings fathers and grandfathers like me to tears. It involves the abducting of young Christian girls. We shudder every time we read news reports that describe Christian family injustice in this land. The stories usually work out this way. Muslim women must marry Muslim men, but Muslim men are allowed to marry any woman they wish with the proviso that any children must be raised as Muslims.

Consequently, in Pakistan, there are Muslim men who often desire some of the very beautiful young Christian girls in the community but realize there is no way their Christian families will agree to the marriage. So, these men resort to abduction. The Christian father's only option is to go to the court where the judge—usually a Muslim—hears the case and pronounces to the Christian father, "Your daughter voluntarily converted to Islam and voluntarily married this Muslim man, so you are to have no more contact with her." One such case involved two young Christian sisters aged thirteen and ten. In this case, the judge allowed the ten-year-old to return home to her family but not the thirteen-year-old.

Safwan, a secret believer in Algeria, found a Christian pamphlet between the paperwork given to him at work and started reading it. Upon discovering him reading the pamphlet, his boss reported him to the police. Later that night the police visited him and searched his entire home. They found Christian CDs, several Christian movies, and a New Testament. "It was clear to them that I had become a Christian. My boss fired me."

STAGE 3: PERSECUTION

"Remember those in prison, as if you were there yourself. Remember also those being mistreated, as if you felt their pain in your own bodies" (Hebrews 13:3).

Rev. Dr Johan Candelin, a former head of the Religious Liberties Commission of the World Evangelical Alliance, said:

If disinformation about any group, including Christians, is disseminated long enough, no one will help when that group is discriminated against because the country has been brainwashed by disinformation. Once discrimination takes place, no one will intervene when persecution comes. When the process gets to [mistreatment], no one will do anything because, "You know they are bad people anyway." As soon as we see the very first case of disinformation, we need to act right away.[81]

Once the first steps in the process occur, mistreatment can be practiced without normal protective measures taking place. Opposition can arise from the state, the police or military, extremist organizations, paramilitary groups, anti-Christian subcultures, and even representatives of other religious groups. The irony is that in many parts of the world, the accusations of the attackers turn the victims into the villains.

This stage is the end result and includes the "big three": torture, imprisonment, and martyrdom. A specific example would be the imprisonment of hundreds of Jesus followers in Eritrea without formal charges—many kept in metal shipping containers.

In Iran, a Christian couple was detained and physically and psychologically tortured for four days. The authorities even threatened to lock up their four-year-old daughter in an "institution." Twenty-eight-year-old Tina Rad from Teheran was arrested and accused of "activities against the holy religion of Islam," because she was reading the Bible with Muslims. Her thirty-one-year-old husband, Makan Arya, was accused of having endangered national security. Both of them had only been Christians for three months. When they were released, the threats started. "If you don't stop with your Jesus, next time we will charge you with apostasy," Tina was told. In Iran, as in some other countries, this can mean the death penalty.

Persecution often comes to Muslim converts who meet together in small groups to talk about the gospel, to grow in the Christian faith, and to encourage one another. They have made a vast transition from Islam to Christianity, and they have a great need of training, security, and a sense of belonging. The church tries to provide for this need and becomes the new "family."

Jamaa Ait Bakrim in Morocco is also serving time for his faith. Moroccan Christians and advocates question the harsh measures of the Muslim state toward a man who dared speak openly about Jesus. An outspoken Christian convert, Bakrim was sentenced to fifteen years in prison for "proselytizing" and destroying "the goods of others" in 2005 after burning two defunct utility poles located in front of his private business in a small town in south Morocco.

Advocates and Moroccan Christians said, however, that the severity of his sentence in relation to his misdemeanour shows that authorities were determined to put him behind bars because he persistently spoke about his faith. "He became a Christian and didn't keep it to himself," said a Moroccan Christian and host for Al Hayat television who goes only by his first name, Rachid, for security reasons. "He shared it with people around him. They will just leave him in the prison, so he dies spiritually and psychologically," said Rachid.

The treatment of Jewish people in Nazi Germany is a good historical example of how these elements can become a persecution process. Adolf Hitler developed a personal hated of Jewish people over his early years. In anti-Semitism, Hitler found an explanation for his failures, a rationalization for his sufferings—the Jews and their supposed conspiracy. The Jews were the single cause of his tensions and humiliation. Hitler adopted this crude, simplistic outlook on life: the Jews are the source of all evil in this world. Hitler thus found a purpose in life, cleansing the German race from the clutches of the Jews. Hatred of the Jews became his obsession, his creed, faith, and religion.

In his speeches and in his writings, Hitler constantly railed against the Jews, citing much disinformation. He often used Martin Luther's writings out of context for support. The Jewish race was to be considered a race of inferior status.

Once he came to power in January 1933, Hitler, pretending to be a Christian, proclaimed the requirement that no persons of Jewish descent could be employed in his government. He declared a boycott of Jewish stores across the country. Signs said, "Germans, protect yourselves! Don't buy from Jews." The stated purpose was stopping the international press, which the Nazis maintained was controlled by the Jews (more disinformation), from printing lies about the Nazi regime. They always cast their aggressions as a defence response to actions against them and the German people. Hitler then also suggested that all pastors with Jewish blood be excluded from church ministry.

Outright public discrimination followed as Hitler legally barred Jews from state-affiliated institutions—even doctors, dentists, lawyers, and university professors. Then Jews were expelled from journalism and the arts. Limits were placed on how many Jewish children could attend public schools. The spouses of Jews were then given the same prohibitions. Next the Jews were officially barred from any involvement in churches. Some pastors were actually converts of Jewish background.

In 1935, the Nuremberg Laws were announced to "protect" the German bloodline:

- Marriages were forbidden between Germans and Jews.
- Extramarital intercourse was forbidden with Jewish people.
- No Jews were allowed to employ German domestic workers under the age of forty-five.
- Jews were forbidden to display German flags but required to display Jewish colours.

Then a law was passed requiring every Jewish person's passport to be emended, adding the name "Israel" for men and "Sarah" for women.

Now that disinformation and discrimination had run its course, Hitler was prepared for full-fledged abuse. In response to an act of violence by a Jewish man in Paris, he gave orders for Jewish homes and businesses to be destroyed and looted; synagogues were set aflame and Jews were beaten and killed. Then Jewish persons were required to wear the yellow star on their sleeves, and soon a full program of eliminating Jewish people began—especially at the hands of the macabre SS squads. The Holocaust had begun and could not be stopped from within.

Awareness of this process in their ethnic history is why many of the loudest voices speaking out against Christian persecution today are Jewish human rights spokespersons.

Just recently, Dr Jordan Peterson told an Israeli audience that when individuals lack moral courage, evil has the opportunity to creep in. He asked, "What do you think happened to Nazi Germany? Do you think individuals lived up to their responsibility? Did they not speak when they should have spoken up? Or did they [just] let the snakes under the carpet turn into terrible, paralyzing, genocidal monsters?"[82]

Christian broadcaster John Loeffler, who is a student of German history, is convinced that the Holocaust in World War II Germany was a clear process that is easily repeatable anywhere and anytime versus any minority group. He identifies a more sophisticated five-stage process which parallels the elements of opposition above:

- Identify
- Marginalize
- Vilify
- Codify (laws)
- Enforce[83]

Dr David Jeremiah in *Is This The End?* goes further and points out a five-element process in the rising slander of the Christian faith in America similar to that proposed and articulated by Msgr Charles Pope[84] and Johnnette Benkovic:

- **Stereotyping.** Christians are stereotyped as ignorant, uneducated, backward, inhibited, homophobic, hateful, and intolerant.
- **Marginalizing.** Christianity is pushed so far to the periphery of society that it is essentially eliminated or at least forced behind closed doors.
- **Threatening.** Individuals lose their jobs for expressing their Christian beliefs and practices.
- **Intimidating.** Cases of loss-of-rights occur regularly against Christians and people are forced into compliance by the government.
- **Litigating.** We can expect lawsuits and court judgements to escalate against Christians who practice their faith.[85]

From a sociological and historical—as well as the biblical—perspective, there are interesting academic parallels.[86]

The good news is that there is another spiral—the upward spiral of the overcomer.

11

THE UPWARD SPIRAL OF OVERCOMING

*Overcomers are not perfect. They fail just
like the rest of us, but they keep on getting
up, keep on repenting, keep on being
willing to surrender themselves to Christ,
and letting Him, who is the only perfect
one, work through them.*

Nancy Missler

The term translated as "overcomer" means one who conquers, prevails, or triumphs. As a verb, it is found twenty-eight times in twenty-four verses in the New Testament. This presupposes and calls attention to the presence of war, contests, battles, and conflicts in humanity's struggle with evil. But it also presupposes that the struggler will win in the end. Thus, it should be no surprise that the greatest number of references or uses of the word are found in the Bible's concluding book of Revelation.

Those whom God refers to as "overcomers" are those who are able to stand witness and maintain their confidence and devotion to God when they find themselves amid the forces of darkness. They are the kind of disciples of Jesus Christ needs for these days when we live in the downward spiral of opposition. I think the best way to highlight the steps of the upward spiral of overcoming is through story.

One of my favorite persons in this life was Chen Mei Bo, a medical doctor in China. English speakers pronounced her Christian name as "Mabel." Her being a senior when I first met her, meant she was always "Aunty Mabel" to me. She was born in 1907 into a Christian family. Her grandfather was a Methodist pastor who was martyred in the Boxer Rebellion of 1900. Her uncle was also a Methodist preacher, and her father was active in the church.

She received her early education at a Methodist girl's school, where she had learned her excellent English. Later, she went to Nanjing University and then took medical studies at Beijing Union Medical College (an extension school of New York University). She graduated in 1934 with an MD—a neurophysiologist. Her classmate in medical school was Dr Esther Li mentioned in chapter 6.

Two years later, she and her best friend, Esther, were converted and baptized. Watchman Nee's wife was their close friend. Both Esther and Mabel had a chance to go to the USA for further studies on a Rockefeller Scholarship to do research but turned it down because God had called them to minister in the interior of China.

During the Japanese occupation, Esther and her husband went to Kunming in southern Yunnan Province and Mabel went with another worker to Tientsin. There at Cheefoo, the Little Flock of Watchman Nee asked her to stay and work with them (Cheefoo is also where Western missionary children were educated). When the war broke out, she moved to the interior of China to minister. By now she had given up her medical career.

This is a good place to pause the story and state the first stage and principle of the upward spiral of overcoming: **1. Assess and know how God has gifted you and what He has called you to do with that gifting.**

I, a prisoner for serving the Lord, beg you to lead a life worthy of your calling, for you have been called by God. Always be humble and gentle. Be patient with each other, making allowance for each other's faults because of your love. Make every effort to keep yourselves united in the Spirit, binding yourselves together with peace. (Ephesians 4:1–3)

Though trained as a doctor, Aunty Mabel realized God was calling her to do missionary work dealing with people's spiritual needs. That didn't mean she would never use the medical training she had received. It helped her many times. When she was ninety years old, she told me that she had never been sick even one day in her long life.

After the war, Mabel returned to Beijing. Her friends were amazed that she had given up her medical practice. She visited all her old classmates to share the gospel with them. Her family was wealthy and lived in a large house in central Beijing (the property on which the Beijing International Hotel now stands).

All that changed abruptly in 1949 when the Communist revolution occurred under the leadership of Chairman Mao Zedong. Her large house marked her out as one of the landlord class. She was evicted from the house and forced to live in a garden shed, with just a stove, two deck chairs, and an old bed. She was forced to go to a "mental" hospital for treatment because she refused to become a Communist and instead spent all her time in Christian ministry. She was later released. Her brother, a music professor, came down with TB. She nursed him for eight years and never married.

The second stage and principle can be clearly seen in Mabel's story: **2. Refuse to let Satan win the battle inside your own head!**

Stay alert! Watch out for your great enemy, the devil. He prowls around like a roaring lion, looking for someone to devour. Stand firm against him, and be strong in your faith. Remember that your family of believers all over the world is going through the same kind of suffering you are. (1 Peter 5:8–9)

Whether it was a challenge about career, or living conditions, or time commitments, or marriage, Mabel did not let Satan make any headway in discouragements or challenges.

Mabel's Christian convictions meant she was an object of suspicion, and so when the Cultural Revolution broke out in the mid-sixties, she was forced to work as a street sweeper like the other "educated" people. But the final indignity was when the Red Guards—young people who were given power to direct the revolution—began to visit her, beating her up, parading her in the streets, and forcing her to wear a placard with her crimes written on it. They put large character posters on her door saying, "She preaches the gospel. She is a counter-revolutionary!" Her personal Bible was taken away. No church meetings or home fellowships were allowed. All Bibles and hymnals were confiscated. She suffered repeated "criticism" meetings and was forced to study the political thought of Mao Zedong.

So thorough were the Red Guards that they erected another large sign outside her humble shed, declaring her a pariah because she had distributed "imperialistic literature," meaning she had given out Bibles in the "mistaken" belief that religion is helpful. For those Red Guards, there was only one "god" allowed, and that was Mao, and only one "Bible" allowed, his little Red Book.

Shunned by neighbours, victimized daily by her work gang, and beaten up regularly by the Red Guards, she came back one night into her little shed and said to God, "I've had enough." She reasoned, "I'm in my sixties now, I've lived a good life, and God will not mind me coming to heaven early." She couldn't bring herself to take her life. She burst into tears and endured another eight years of beatings, isolation, and victimization.

Mabel says, "The Cultural Revolution touched the soul of every person. But the Christian has a secret place with the Lord that no one can touch … I gave my fears to Jesus and somehow, God gave me the strength to endure."

It is not hard to see the third stage and principle here: **3. Turn over all your fears to Jesus!**

I am leaving you with a gift—peace of mind and heart. And the peace I give is a gift the world cannot give. So don't be troubled or afraid. (John 14:27)

In the late 1970s, after Mao died and Deng Xiaoping returned to power, China began to put the excesses of the Cultural Revolution behind. The hated Red Guards were disbanded, and the Little Red Book fell into disuse. Mabel was not restored to her large family house. However, she began to receive a stream of visitors in her newly assigned nearby small apartment. To her astonishment, many of these visitors were high-ranking members of the Communist Party. Even more astonishingly, they asked her for Bibles.

"Why come to me out of all the people in Beijing? Why do you come to the house of a seventy-year-old?" she would ask. Each would answer the same, "During the Cultural Revolution, there was a large sign outside your house listing your crimes. One of them was that you had distributed Bibles. So I'm here on the chance that you might have one left."

Amazingly, that sign which had made her life such a misery became the means of a new ministry. It kept people away from her during the Cultural Revolution, but afterwards, after she had endured, it drew them in. Mabel was able to contact Open Doors and became the first conduit of Scriptures into China's capital. She became a vital supplier, and a number of high-ranking members of the Communist Party in China today owe their faith to her endurance.

She reflected, "It's been nice to know why. It helps my faith. But it was hard. Every day was hard. I can't say I saw Jesus or even felt Him close most of the time. I just got the strength from Him to keep going, and that was enough."

Stage and principle number four: **4. Keep pressing on with patient endurance!**

Patient endurance is what you need now, so that you will continue to do God's will. Then you will receive all that he has promised. (Hebrews 10:36)

I met Aunty Mabel personally for the first time when she was eighty-eight years young. I had heard she had a special burden for the most unreached people group in China—the Tibetans. She has been on mission trips there twice and was planning to go again. She was well over ninety when she made that third mission trip. This was her favourite subject and burning passion.

My lifelong friend and travelling buddy, Dr Jim Cunningham, and I were in Beijing leading a Canadian/USA Christian tour group soon to be heading up the mountains to Lhasa, Tibet. I telephoned Aunty Mabel and asked if we could meet. She quickly replied, "Oh yes, meet me at my favourite restaurant, McDonald's." There was only one in the center of the city at the time. "I love cheeseburgers and chocolate milkshakes."

We were overwhelmed by this small-framed, tiny eighty-eight-year-old woman with the big smile who walked faster than we in our early fifties did. As we all enjoyed her "special" meal order, she shared how God had kept her healthy all her long life. It helped us enjoy the cheeseburgers and milkshakes even more.

After hearing her life story, we asked about her mission trips to Tibet. She told about planting two house churches in the capital city. "Oh, the Lord has put this group of unreached people on my heart," she blurted. "They are such spiritually needy people. Tibet is the darkest spot in the world. But God is building His church even there.

"I'm going back there next month on another mission trip. Please pray for me. Last time I fainted from the thin air up there. And my nose bled frequently. But I'm committed to go there and shine for Jesus.

"At the fellowship of believers in the capital, I taught them to sing, 'He Is Lord' and 'I Have Decided to Follow Jesus, No Turning Back.' We need to reach more people for Jesus. He is saying to us, 'You need to hurry and get the job done, so I can come back again!' But the only way to win them is one-by-one."

Mabel was such an inspiration. When she learned I had worked all through the 1970s with Far East Broadcasting in Manila, she said. "I listen to the English service all the time. My favourite program is *In Touch* with Dr Charles Stanley from Atlanta, Georgia, USA. Do you know Dr Stanley?"

"Never met him personally," I replied. But a few years later, I took a picture for them of their faithful listener, Mabel, when I shared in their chapel time at the *In Touch* office in Atlanta.

Her life's focus is: Love God more than anything or anyone! She quickly adds, "The official Three-Self Church here in China asks you to love your country above all."

Mabel spent all her time discipling new believers and distributing Bibles. But on December 30, 1991, the police came to her home and confiscated the many Bibles and other spiritual books in her apartment. They told her that China would provide all the books needed for any group. But the police overlooked a VHS copy of the movie *Jesus*, which Christian visitors had brought her.

She muttered to herself as she stomped down the road. Her hurried steps were more impatient than usual. The sidewalk shopkeepers and food servers observed her gait and thought she was angry or worried. But the faint smile on Mabel's face belied her body language.

The only thing different about this trip down her dusty city street was the *Jesus* video in her hand. She held it close to herself like a treasure chest.

Lord, please let my plan work, she telegraphed.

The bright sunshine made her greying hair seem whiter than usual.

Mabel's blood was still boiling from the Public Security Bureau raid on her home earlier that day.

"We will always be watching," they had taunted her.

She turned the corner to the left when she reached the main thoroughfare. She could now see her destination two long blocks down this wide tree-lined boulevard. Mabel began to rehearse again what she would say on arrival.

Lord, please help me to keep a positive attitude, she prayed again.

The young lady at the desk looked askance in her direction.

"I want to talk to the chief of police!" Mabel demanded firmly.

Mabel's soft face and gentle spirit appealed to the receptionist. But she put up her normal false front.

"He's very busy right now. Do you have an appointment?"

"No. But today his men were at my house, and they did not see this," she said, waving the videotape in the air.

The receptionist was puzzled. Why would this lady volunteer such information?

As though in obedience to a master, she ushered Mabel into the police chief's office. He acted oblivious to her arrival yet grunted a question of intent.

"Sir," Mabel began slowly, "earlier today your men raided my house and took all the Bibles I had stored there. I understand that they were just doing their job. But after they left, I noticed that they missed this videotape. I need to know from you if this is acceptable material or not. Would you and your staff check it for me?"

At first, the chief's response was disgust. Yet the sincerity in her voice and on her face prodded him to give it a second thought.

"Very well, come back in two weeks," he muttered, dismissing her with a wave of the hand.

Mabel almost skipped out the door with overflowing joy as she headed toward home. *Thank You, Lord! How else could I get the chief of police with his staff to watch Jesus?*

As she now strolled homeward, she recounted how God had given her witness opportunities all her long life. From the time of her conversion as a young woman and subsequent friendship with Watchman Nee's wife, she had turned down study and career advancement opportunities to be a missionary in interior China. She made sure she visited all her university classmates to share the gospel with them. They were now successful medical doctors.

Mabel smiled as she remembered just how fruitful her own missionary work had been during the Japanese occupation and the war years that followed. So much so that she had given up her medical career.

"Lord, You do all things well!" she whispered. "And thanks to You, I haven't had one day of sickness in my eighty-plus years."

Suddenly a transient thought raced through her active memory. She immediately spun her body to the left and headed west.

Oh, I promised Pastor Allen that I would join him for dinner with some foreign guests tonight, she mused. *I almost forgot! But I must be home by nine to hear my favourite program on FEBC radio!*

She spotted them as soon as she entered the hotel dining room. Pastor Allen was busy sharing his long testimony of God's faithfulness as she approached the round table. The conversation halted as introductions were made all around and she gracefully took her place. She quickly shared her mixed emotions with him and the group about what had happened to her that day.

"The Lord is making the situation here such that you have to depend on the Holy Spirit. Please pray for the chief of police. Pray that he and his staff will watch the video and want to know and follow Jesus!" she concluded.

"Where did you learn such good English, Mabel?" the group leader asked.

"I went to a Methodist girl's school run by missionaries many years ago."

Pastor Allen was asked to continue his story of long-term imprisonment during the Cultural Revolution.

"And what happened to you during this time, Mabel?" the leader asked again.

Mabel hesitated. She did not even want to relive the horrible memories. But she knew it would encourage the group to hear another testimony of God's faithfulness in helping her persevere.

"During the Cultural Revolution, all church meetings and home fellowships were closed. All Bibles and hymnals were confiscated. Anyone with an education received extra harsh treatment. Because I was trained as a medical doctor, I was forced to work as a street sweeper like other educated people. And because I was known for the fellowship held in my home, the Red Guards came and took away my personal Bible. They treated me very badly and then posted large character posters on my door. Every day I was subjected to repeated 'criticism' meetings and forced to study the political thought of Mao Zedong. It hurts to even think about that time. I was supposed to save my 'soul' through reforming my way of thinking.

"It always impressed me that in his writings Mao, though himself a Communist, often referred to the saving of a person's 'soul.' During the Cultural Revolution, 'soul' was mentioned frequently. In speeches made from Tiananmen Square, the Red Guards were often encouraged to allow the revolutionary spirit to touch their 'souls' in order to improve themselves. The Cultural Revolution touched the 'soul' of every person. But the Christian has a secret place with the Lord that no one can touch!"

Mabel concluded, "What I can say about my Christian walk with Jesus is simply this: Love the Lord more than anyone or anything! The government church asks you to love your country above all else. We, Chinese believers, have paid a price to follow Jesus. But we can still pay much more."

The group of visitors had been quickly taking notes. Now they just looked at each other and shook their heads as though in disbelief.

Mabel's quick question snapped them out of this response. "Has any of you been to Lhasa, Tibet?"

They all shook their heads.

"Oh, the Lord has put this group of unreached people on my heart." She continued, "They are such spiritually needy people. Tibet is the darkest spot in the world. But God is building His church even in Tibet. I'm going back there on another mission trip. Please pray for me."

Her excitement made her sentences seem disjointed. By now the group leader could not contain himself. "Don't you Chinese Christians ever retire?" he blurted.

Pastor Allen, also an octogenarian, interrupted. "Retire! Where do you read about that in the Bible?"

Again, the group shook their heads, this time with a ripple of laughter.

"No," Pastor Allen continued, "Jesus said, 'Work while it is yet day, for the night is coming when no man can work!'"

Mabel interjected, "I need to get home now. I'm expecting another visitor tonight. A young lady from Inner Mongolia is coming for a discipleship class. She just received Jesus last week.

"But before I go, please let me leave some prayer requests with you. Please pray for the many lost souls here in China. Pray for the many Bibles and training materials needed by the fast-growing church here. And also pray that more Sauls will be turned into Pauls! I'm referring to government leaders coming to know Jesus."

Mabel said her farewells and was prepared to walk home. But the group would hear nothing of it. They ultimately prevailed on her to at least let them hire a taxi to take her home.

She knew something was different as soon as she walked into her apartment.

"Hi, Aunty Mabel," said Greg bounding around the corner in his colourful sarong. "I let myself in—as usual. There is a young lady here waiting for you too. I couldn't understand her accented Mandarin."

"Greg," responded Mabel with a hug, "I didn't expect you until tomorrow! What happened?"

"I thought I'd surprise you since I returned a day early from Vietnam!"

"The taxi driver just prayed outside to receive the Lord!" she joyfully exploded changing the subject. "He had been listening to Christian radio broadcasts and I simply encouraged him to pray the sinner's prayer—and he did!"

"Praise the Lord! And who is this young lady waiting here?"

"Oh, she's a new believer. Came to our city all the way from Inner Mongolia. She really needs the fullness of the Holy Spirit. Let me spend an hour with her and then we'll have some tea. I want to hear all about your trip to Vietnam!"

"By the way, take any Bibles you brought for me over to Pastor Allen's place right away. Be careful. They're watching! Everything I had here was confiscated earlier today."

Mabel had already forgotten about her favourite Christian radio broadcast now being aired from FEBC Manila. Before long she and Greg—a tall, blond Aussie—were deep in conversation. Even though it was officially discouraged, Greg loved to stay at Mabel's apartment on his short visits to China. She was such an inspiration. He shared at length the exciting growth of believers in Vietnam as well as the shortage of Bibles and spiritual books and training materials.

"Sounds like here in China!" she softly interjected.

Mabel sat in rapt attention as Greg explained how new believers in one Vietnamese house church network memorize Psalm 119 in order to get on the list of those approved to receive a Bible when they are available.

"Oh Greg!" she responded with deep emotion. "Those believers in Vietnam need to have God's Word."

She began to fumble with the money belt at her waistline and pulled out three hundred yuan. "This is all the money I have, Greg. But I want you to take it and buy Bibles for those new believers in Vietnam!"

Many of the details of this story I learned from Aunty Mabel's niece who lived in Scarborough, Ontario. Though a simple lady living a simple lifestyle,

Aunty Mabel is a testimony of God's goodness over a long, joyful lifetime. She lived to age ninety-nine and continued to be a fearless witness for Jesus to the very end. Today she's at the very top of the upward spiral—in heaven with Jesus enjoying her eternal reward.

Stage and principle number five: **5. Keep faithfully moving forward in discipleship and stewardship one step at a time until you meet Jesus face-to-face.**

> We do this [run the race with endurance] by keeping our eyes on Jesus, the champion who initiates and perfects our faith. Because of the joy awaiting him, he endured the cross, disregarding its shame. Now he is seated in the place of honor beside God's throne. (Hebrews 12:2)

Keeping your eyes, thoughts, and life fixed on Jesus enables you to join the upward spiral of the overcomer.

12
CONTEMPORARY PERSPECTIVES

Leave the irreparable past behind and step
forth into the invincible future.
Oswald Chambers

There have been some very excellent books and articles written on this topic in recent years. In this chapter, I will give a brief overview of some of the writings I have benefitted from reading.

THE BENEDICT OPTION
The Benedict Option written by Christian commentator, Rod Dreher, is what I call a conscious choice by orthodox Christians to secede, more or less, from the modern world—even if we stay geographically in place—and to cultivate practices and communities in which it is possible to live out the faith together, with resiliency and joy. It is a kind of deliberate, strategic retreat so that we can tend our own gardens and cultivate the deep roots that our kids and their kids, and great grandkids will need to hold on to the faith through the darker times ahead.

Dreher describes what this might look like in our times. His concept is taken from Saint Benedict, the famous founder of a major monastic order of old who established independent communities of believers preserving virtue, literacy, and civilization through the Dark Ages.

An Eastern Orthodox believer, Dreher is not proposing we don habits and cloister ourselves in monasteries. But he is proposing that we recognize our civilization's decline, disentangle Christian identity from secular culture, and prepare the church to preserve that identity for future generations. He writes,

The time is going to come when we Christians will have to separate from the mainstream—not head for the hills … but live in some sort of separate community so we can be the church. Not so we can keep ourselves pure but so that we can remind ourselves of who we are and be a light to the world, called to fidelity to Christ.[87]

Some of his proposals are in the areas of Christian community building, home education, intentional biblical studies especially focussing on the Christian view of sex and sexuality that counter our culture's materialism and consumerism, redoubled support for Christian legal defence organizations, and careful restriction of secular media and technology consumption.

THE WILBERFORCE OPTION

How do we live this way in an increasingly antagonistic culture? Christian writers Michael Gerson and Peter Wehner promote "the Wilberforce Option." William Wilberforce was a British politician, philanthropist, and leader of the movement to abolish the slave trade.

The authors say in their *Christianity Today* article:

William Wilberforce, the greatest political enemy of the 19th-century slave trade, believed Christians should be the first to respond to social injustices. Along with other prominent Christians of his era, Wilberforce made Christian commitment synonymous with defending human rights against powerful social interests …

For most of the past 2,000 years, Christians have lived in societies that haven't generally reflected their values, particularly their sexual values. It was assumed, certainly by Jesus and his disciples, that "resident alien" is a natural position for a Christian … Christianity's greatest period of vulnerability and political weakness was the time of its most explosive growth. It became a magnet to others as well as a model of compassion.[88]

Like Wilberforce, rather than only lecturing the world, which he did with significant influence, we need to also show a different and better way to live in the world, which includes following the teaching of the prophet Jeremiah. He told his people not to lose heart but to get busy building houses and planting gardens as well as seeking "the welfare of the city where I sent you into exile" (Jeremiah 29:7).

When enough of us openly stand up for what is good and right in our communities, we can create a movement, no matter how slowly it grows, that can ultimately make a difference. Wilberforce died just three days after hearing that the anti-slavery act he sponsored passed in Parliament. His goals took a lifetime but ultimately triumphed.

THE DR KING OPTION

Pastor Gabriel Salguero, president of the National Latino Evangelical Coalition, while agreeing that the Wilberforce Option is better than angry combativeness or disillusioned withdrawal, argues that Wilberforce still operated in cultural engagement that depended on power and privilege. Although Salguero overlooks that Wilberforce had to get elected first, and then used his position for good.

He writes,

There is another option, named after another transformational Christian leader who did not arise from privilege and position: "the Dr. King Option." Martin Luther King Jr.'s commitment to nonviolent advocacy, coupled with service, won the hearts and minds of many Americans.

King's public and civil advocacy, coupled with a willingness to serve the most vulnerable, brought genuine transformation. Though he did not possess all the markers of power, he brought doctoral-level training and broad cultural experience to his philosophical personalism and commitment to the dignity of all people.

Any theory of evangelical public engagement has much to learn from King, America's most effective prophet. He was part of a grassroots movement that included people of every race—intellectuals, actors, lawyers, artists, college students, mothers and fathers. *The movement's power was not in its social location but rather in its gospel commitment to truth, love, and service.*

The Dr. King Option is neither passive nor power-hungry; it seeks to transform and heal culture while maintaining its own soul. If evangelicals of all cultures can learn from this black preacher from Georgia, our Christian witness and cultural engagement could inspire a new generation.[89] (Emphasis mine.)

THE JEREMIAH OPTION

Dr David Jeremiah suggests that followers of Jesus responding to the pressures and squeeze of aggressive secularism need to understand the benefits of suffering and then take some action steps.

He reminds us that biblically we learn that suffering promotes character and character provokes courage. Suffering also proves godliness in that suffering for Christ is a sure sign we are living for Christ. As well, suffering can produce joy as in the case of Paul and Silas in the Philippian jail and the apostles in Acts who rejoiced when they were counted worthy of suffering shame for the name of Jesus. Finally, suffering helps us look to the future rewards God has promised.

Based on these principles, here are his three recommended action steps:

• Determine to stand for the truth.

• Draw support from one another.

• Derive your security from the Lord.

Remember to whom we belong and do not be afraid. God gives courage to His faithful people to stand strong! In that strength, Dr Jeremiah also appeals to his fellow Americans to trust God and pray for spiritual and moral revival for the nation. Revival is crucial to bring about unity and mutual concern for others in an extremely fragmented and angry society which exhibits fits of violence and threats of violence even against our leaders.

THE NYQUIST OPTION

Dr J. Paul Nyquist was the president of the renowned Moody Bible College in Chicago in 2015 when he wrote his book, *Prepare: Living Your Faith in an Increasingly Hostile Culture*.[90] He is a student of the Bible and an insightful scholar on the topic of Christian persecution. He has thoroughly studied Glenn Penner's monumental biblical theology of persecution and discipleship, *In the Shadow of the Cross*.[91]

Dr Nyquist, like Penner, realizes the distinct connection between Christian persecution and Christian discipleship. Penner's slogan is "The cross-bearing message requires cross-bearing messengers." Nyquist expands this to say, "The American church has missed a vital element of discipleship. Important spiritual formation cannot be realized without experiencing suffering. Without this suffering, perseverance in the face of hardship remains theoretical."[92] And when he discusses Jesus's ultimate call to discipleship in Matthew 16:24–27 in taking up our cross daily, he adds, "Without an environment of persecution we often fail to understand the extreme commitment Jesus requires of his disciples."[93]

The clarion call of Scripture and history is for followers of Jesus to respond to the challenges of their culture with courage and as Jesus himself exhibited, a life also filled with grace and truth. Nyquist proposes we live out what he calls five counter-intuitive biblical principles regarding persecution:

- **Normal, not strange.** If we want to display godliness as a fully devoted disciple of Christ, we can expect to be persecuted.
- **Blessed, not cursed.** Persecution brings "blessing" because it allows us to know Christ more and become more like Him.
- **Exposed, not protected.** We shouldn't rely on family or government to defend us when persecution comes.
- **Compassion, not anger.** The most powerful apologetic is the faithful lives of God's people, demonstrating love, faith and hope in the midst of a hostile world.
- **Rewarded, not forgotten.** Our God will remember all we've done and everything we've sacrificed, and He'll abundantly reward us.

These points are well worth the reading and studying. A late chapter documents the persecution against Christians in Pakistan and responses to it. He concludes that there is hope for the future for all of us which comes from God's help. "The stormy blast is coming. Be prepared. And remember—God will help us."[94]

DIGITAL BABYLON OPTION

David Kinnaman and Mark Matlock decry the crisis era in which we live and label it "digital Babylon." In their book, *Faith for Exiles: 5 Ways for a New Generation to Follow Jesus in Digital Babylon*, Babylon is characterized as a culture set against the purposes of God—a human society that glorified pride, power, prestige, and pleasure.[95]

The authors identify four kinds of exiles among young people who were raised as Christians: prodigals (22%), nomads (30%), habitual churchgoers (38%), and resilient disciples (10%).

Kinnaman and Matlock are also impressed with Jeremiah in the Bible and his dealings with those in Israel who would be experiencing the coming exile:

- Pray for the peace and prosperity of the city in which you'll live in exile.
- Live in faithfulness to God and in holiness.
- Live fruitful lives; in other words, plan to stay.
- Live for the sake of others.
- Be wary, realistic, and hopeful.
- Take epic risks to say and do what is right.
- Realize that God is at work for good, even in exile.
- Look wholeheartedly for God and He will be found.

Their five suggested practices for exiles who desire to be significant are:

- To form a resilient identity, experience intimacy with Jesus.
- In a complex and anxious age, develop the muscles of cultural discernment.
- When isolation and mistrust are the norms, forge meaningful, intergenerational relationships.
- To ground and motivate an ambitious generation, train for vocational discipleship.
- Curb entitlement and self-centered tendencies by engaging in counter-cultural mission.[96]

They conclude, "Exiles are instrumental to God's purposes. During times of major change and intense pressure, exiles show the way forward. Exiles help to reform and revitalize the church, reorienting it toward God. A faith for exiles represents hope for the church."[97]

These are practices we all can engage in as a way to live at the crossroads of culture and Christian faith.

HOPE OF NATIONS: NINE MANIFESTOS OPTION

Like the wine at the Cana wedding feast, I have left the best to the end. In the extremely insightful book, *Hope of Nations: Standing Strong in a Post-Truth, Post-Christian World*, John S. Dickerson points out nine post-Christian trends we currently face:

- A world that is post-Christian
- A world that is post-truth
- A world that is post-knowledge
- A world that is post-church
- A world that is post-decency
- A world that is post-human

- A world that is post-prosperity
- A world that is post-liberty
- A world that is post-peace[98]

I greatly appreciated Pastor Dickerson's treatise because he focuses his conclusions on how we are to live in the face of these current challenges and hopelessness, in light of what we can and cannot control. He proposes nine excellent biblical parallel manifestos:

- In a world where truth is feelings-based, **we will remain rooted to the Christian Scriptures** and their life-giving direction.
- In a society of educated ignorance and blindness, **we will train our young** in the freedom, knowledge, and power of Christian truth.
- In a world where Christians are labelled as bigots or backward, **we will be known for doing good**, serving the least of these and loving our neighbours.
- In a world where people are treated as commodities or as opponents, **we will dignify all people as image bearers of God.**
- In a post-Christian world, **we will be ambassadors** to foreign tribes, behaving diplomatically to neighbours who have been told the worst about Christianity.
- In a world where opponents are vilified and crucified, **we will love our persecutors**.
- In a world competing for limited resources, driven by fear, unrest, and scarcity, **we will remain calm,** confident that our Father provides our daily bread.
- In a world where we are discriminated against, prejudged, and even persecuted, **we will be invincible** as we serve God's purposes for which we are placed here, now.
- In a world divided by violence, terrorism, and war, **we will be fearless**.[99]

These nine commitments are perceptive and valuable for Jesus followers wanting to live a balanced life like Jesus of grace and truth. Highlight them and memorize them. But above all, live them!

13
THE WOLF LIES DOWN WITH THE LAMB

We will have all eternity to celebrate the victories, but only a few hours before sunset to win them.

Amy Carmichael

Isaiah's picture of the future new earth reveals the wolf and the lamb eating peacefully together (Isaiah 65:25). The broken world's discord has been corrected.

Earlier, in Isaiah 11:6, people have often misquoted the passage as the lion will lie down with the lamb. But literally it says, the wolf will lie down—or live together—with the lamb. The word picture Isaiah painted about the coming new order in this passage ends with the statement, "and a little child will lead them all." What a glorious day that will be!

Meanwhile, we live as lambs among wolves in a very broken world. Jesus realized this and challenged us to be as trusting and obedient as little children as well as salt and light as we live out our lives for Him through the power of His Holy Spirit.

Hopefully you have clearly seen through Scripture and story the need for, and the ability to live, a balanced life of grace and truth—as Dr Martin Luther King Jr expressed it, developing "a tough mind and a tender heart." His life principle resonates with the perspective we have been exploring together: "Life at its best is a creative synthesis of opposites in fruitful harmony." Who doesn't want to live their best life? Contemplate that for a while. It is simple yet profound.

From my decades of ministry and observations, I conclude with a summary of primary principles relating to this perspective for those wanting to live "the Jesus way" and become one of Os Guinness's "impossible people."

1. Don't let it surprise you. Expect opposition (1 Peter 4:12–14). Opposition and suffering are to be anticipated with an awareness that it does not interfere with God's plan for us. (Read Andrew Brunson's comments in Appendix A).

2. Evaluate the opposition you are receiving. Is it because of your own words and actions or Jesus (in you)?

3. Use the SEE, JUDGE, ACT model mentioned in Chapter 6, to look around you and see what might prompt you to courageously stand up for religious freedom or against tyranny.

4. Decide when and how to ACT (with grace) in response to the preceding step.

5. Understand Satan's tactics of deceit and intimidation. Conquer the fears he perpetrates—especially the fear of death. Resist him and he will run! Be willing to take risks.

6. Regularly rehearse the biblical ways Jesus expects us to respond to opposition and challenges. Listen to the Holy Spirit who has promised to give us the right words when we need them. Jesus did not return insult for insult. He did not threaten. He did not ask for revenge on those who wronged Him. He loved them and prayed for them. He said bless those who curse you, love those who hate you, pray for those who persecute you, and do good to those who mistreat you.

7. Practice "grace" exchanges among your family members and circle of friends. This will help your responses when confronted by direct opposition from outside your inner circle.

8. Make daily recommitment to retaliate the third way—not as the world retaliates—but respond with non-violence and aggressive love no matter how severe the opposition. Learn the lessons from the persecuted church around the world.

9. Regardless of the size of your current church fellowship, establish a small group or network of proven trustworthy spiritual brothers and

sisters you can meet with, pray with, and trust to be kindred spirits when things get difficult.

10. Prepare your family (home and church)—especially children and grandchildren—to withstand the attacks of the culture. This point is eloquently made by internet blogger Jack Lee:

We should begin praying now about these realities for churches and families. It's time to prepare our children for a culture that will hate them for their faith. I read a quote recently (regretfully, I do not recall who said it) that said in so many words *if we are not proactively preparing our families to withstand the attacks of the culture, they will be assimilated into it.* Not possibly assimilated but certainly; as in, it will happen. We must speak boldly, honestly, and directly to our children and fellow Christians about the dangers of the sexual revolution and the changing world. These are not just the ramblings of some internet blogger; remember, such things are promised to us in Scripture.

Christian, align your thinking with that of Scripture and remind yourself of surety in our Savior. Consider together the numerous times in the Old Testament how God purged sin from his people. God has often used persecution as a means of purifying and growing His church. Church Father Tertullian once famously said that "the blood of the martyrs is the seed of the Church" (*Apologeticus*, Chapter 50). After the purging fires of persecution, what remains will be pure gold.

While it is the time to start preparing our churches, families, and hearts for persecution, it is not time to fret. God will be with His people. Regardless of any changing political landscape, God reigns. [North] America is not eternal. It is a nation and one day it will fall. Its buildings, monuments, and ideas will perish. Be warned but do not be discouraged. Our God is mighty and preserves His own.[100]

When the storms of life come upon us—and all of us will experience them—we can rise above them by setting our minds on God and our eyes on Jesus and walking by faith and not by sight. God enables us to ride the winds of the storm like an eagle. Remember, it is not the burdens of life that weigh us down, it is how we handle them.

Be a lamb among the wolves. Stay close to the Shepherd. Live the balanced life of grace and truth!

PREPARE TO STAND

WHEN GOD'S GRACE ISN'T WHAT WE EXPECTED

By Andrew Brunson

In a new video series, Andrew Brunson warns the church that "a dark tidal wave is on the horizon. It's a wave of hostility and persecution that is about to crash onto the church." Brunson knows persecution firsthand, having been imprisoned for two years in Turkey because of his Christian faith. In this first of a seven-part series adapted from the videos, Brunson explains how we can begin to prepare, so when persecution comes, we will stand firm to the end.

My wife, Norine, and I lived in Turkey for 25 years, starting churches and a house of prayer, and working with refugees. Our lives were turned upside down one day when we were invited to the local police station and told that there was an order to arrest and deport us.

The problem is, they never got around to deporting us. They released Norine after two weeks, but they held me for two years. They accused me of being a military spy, a terrorist, and of trying to overthrow the Turkish government.

None of this was true. They wanted to make an example of someone in order to intimidate other Christians, and they chose me. They threatened to give me three life sentences in solitary confinement.

I thought of myself as a relatively tough missionary—we had faced threats before; I had even been shot at once. But I was not prepared for what I experienced in prison. It was much more difficult than I imagined it would be, and I almost didn't make it through. Persecution almost knocked me out.

Many Christians do not think this can happen in the United States, but it can. Followers of Jesus throughout history and in countries around the world have experienced persecution. In fact, our experience of very little persecution up to now is the exception.

I think everyone can see that our society has changed significantly in the last generation or two.

The commanding heights of our culture—the corporate world, big tech, arts, media, entertainment, professional sports, schools and universities, government bureaucracy—are mostly populated by people who do not honor God. In fact, many openly defy Him. These are the people who control the centers of power and influence. They have the platforms to amplify their voices and shape public opinion, and they're increasingly hostile to those who identify clearly with Jesus and His teaching.

I'm not talking about politics. I'm not thinking of this as an issue of right versus left, but rather followers of Jesus on the one hand, and on the other, those who are hostile to followers of Jesus.

WHAT WILL DRIVE PERSECUTION

I think two wedge issues will drive persecution. First, the exclusivity of Jesus in salvation—that Jesus is the only way to God. Second, that Jesus demands obedience from His followers in a number of areas that are hotly contested in our culture, such as sexual morality, gender identity, marriage, family, life and Biblical justice. Those who are faithful to Jesus in upholding Gospel exclusivity and obedience to Christ are going to be labeled as evil people, and those who persecute us will justify themselves by saying that we are a people of hate, that we carry a message of hate.

This, of course, is completely backward. It's a satanic lie. But think of Jesus. He was the most loving and kind man in history, and yet people called Him evil. They said He was demonic, and an angry mob demanded He be killed in a gruesome way. And Jesus said that just as the world hated Him, it will also hate His followers.

And that's true. Christians are the most persecuted religious group in the world. Why? It's because when we walk closely with Jesus, we carry His scent, and people react to Him in us.

I think this is some of what will happen: Many, in the name of being inclusive and tolerant, will say that the followers of Jesus are a threat to safety. They'll say: "You can't work here. Your views make people feel unsafe. You can't use social media. You can't use our financial products. We won't process your payments. We're canceling your bank account. You can't use these credit cards. And as for your church, we're closing down your website and your podcasts. And we're stripping you of your tax-exempt status because you have a message of hate."

These are some of the possible pressure points. I don't know how far it will go, but even if it's just being despised and hated and slandered, that can be difficult enough.

For now, we still have robust legal protections for freedom of religion, but as the commanding heights of our culture turn against our Judeo-Christian heritage, these protections can erode very quickly. And when we reach a tipping point, it will accelerate rapidly across a wide front.

The majority of believers are not ready for the pressures of persecution, and this is very dangerous. I can tell you this from personal experience. I came close to failing, especially during my first year in prison. At times I was suicidal. I was overcome with fear and despair. I went into relational crisis with God.

I believe one of the purposes God had in my imprisonment was that I would learn how to stand under pressure even when I was weak and overwhelmed, and this was in part so that I could encourage others to stand when they're under pressure.

In this series I will highlight some of the spiritual dangers ahead and suggest some steps we can take to prepare ourselves to stand. This is not a comprehensive list, but these are things that I learned and practiced that helped me to endure under intense pressure, and I believe they will help you also.

I'm focusing on preparation of the heart, which is the most important and fundamental factor in determining whether we will stand faithful. And that is the ultimate goal: to be faithful to the end.

TALK AND PLAN

Here's how we can start to prepare to stand under pressure: We need to talk about persecution, be aware of it and plan for it. It needs to be on our radar screen, and I say this especially for pastors, leaders, influencers, parents and grandparents, because you have people under your care. If we don't talk about it, then when that dark wave hits, it is going to shock many people, and that places them in danger of being knocked out.

This is especially true because persecution is different from other trials. There are many pressures that we cannot easily escape—an illness, grief from a loss, a broken relationship. But persecution is different because the pressure will usually stop if you just compromise. This is why we must prepare ourselves ahead of time, so that when pressure comes and we are afraid, we do not run but stand firm. Here are three practical things to do.

Read in a New Way

First, read the New Testament with a different eye. It's full of exhortations to prepare and also examples of people living victoriously under persecution. In prison, I especially read 2 Timothy, which Paul wrote in a dungeon before he was martyred. The letter of 1 Peter addresses Christians who are suffering for doing good. Read the Gospels with a focus on what Jesus says about persecution, how He Himself deals with persecution and how He prepares His disciples. Discuss with your loved ones and decide now that "as for me and my house, we will serve the Lord" (Joshua 24:15)—even if it becomes costly.

Pray for Strength

Second, begin to pray now that you and your loved ones will have enough faith and strength to stand. This is what Jesus urged His disciples to do. He said, "Watch and pray so that you will not fall into temptation. The spirit is willing, but the flesh is weak" (Matthew 26:41 NIV). And Peter says to believers facing persecution, "Be sober-minded; be watchful. Your adversary the devil prowls around like a roaring lion, seeking someone to devour" (1 Peter 5:8).

Learn From Persecuted Believers

Third, learn from persecuted Christians, those who have gone before and endured faithfully. We have been conditioned not to expect persecution in this country, so we need to change our mindset. This is not a time for ministry as usual in the church. Many churches are looking at how to expand, but very few are getting ready for the wave that is about to hit. Some of my friends are expecting a revival, and I hope it comes. But before we see revival fire, I think we will go through a refining fire. So, we need to prioritize preparing ourselves right now.

Early in my detention, my mother was allowed to visit me, and she said to me, "Andrew, there's a long line of people who have suffered for Jesus Christ. My son, it is now your turn to stand in that line." This was a difficult thing to hear, but it was the right perspective. Accept that you may have to stand in that line.

THE HARD TRUTH

The hard truth is that God allows His children to suffer persecution, and it can be more difficult than we think. I had an idealistic view of how I would handle intense persecution like imprisonment. And looking back, I think it would have helped me to know how difficult it can be, so that I could adjust my mindset and expectations.

I hear some people saying confidently now, "Persecution will be good for us. It will build the church. Bring it on." We need to be careful not to be over-confident. I say to you again, it can be more difficult than we think, and God's faithfulness, His help, His grace, may look different than what we would expect.

Let me give you a couple of examples. Paul declared confidently to Timothy: "The Lord will rescue me from every evil deed and bring me safely into His heavenly Kingdom" (2 Timothy 4:18). But when he wrote this, he was suffering in a miserable Roman dungeon. He was expecting to be executed, so safety and being rescued may look different than we imagined. And Jesus tells His disciples that they're going to face persecution and be hated by everybody. Some of them will be imprisoned. Some of them will be put to death. And then after giving them this long list of terrible things that can happen to them, He says, "But not a hair of your head will perish" (Luke 21:18). So, escaping harm may not look the way we expect.

THE SUPREMACY OF JESUS

Because this can be a discouraging subject, we need to keep before us the truth of the supremacy of Jesus, the image of Jesus as the Lion. He will not be defeated.

C.S. Lewis in "The Chronicles of Narnia" tells the story of a horse and his boy who want to go to Narnia. But to get there, they have to undertake a perilous journey that's filled with hardship and danger. One of the key points in the book is when the boy and the horse have to go through a very dangerous mountain area at night. It's dark. They can't see anything and there are sheer cliffs. But the great lion, Aslan, takes them through to the other side.

A year before I was arrested, someone had referred to this story when praying over us, and said that I had a perilous journey ahead of me, but that I would press through, that I would keep going, because God would be with me. And we wrote that down.

Right before we were arrested, Norine happened to grab this prayer among some other random pages as she left our home in a flurry on her way to a prayer retreat. In God's timing, this is what she was praying through right before my perilous journey began. I thought of it often in prison. There was hardship. There was real danger, and at times I came close to defeat. What God wanted to highlight for me was the Lion—the Lion of Judah, Jesus Christ. He was there and would take me through to the other side.

My brothers and sisters, we are on a perilous journey. There will be hardship and danger, but the Lion is with us. At some point, the journey will end, and it will end in victory for the Lion and for those who are on His side.

_____

This article is adapted from the video series "Prepare to Stand," by Andrew Brunson. Brunson serves as special advisor for religious freedom at Family Research Council.

_____

For more than 65 years, Open Doors has worked in the most oppressive and restrictive countries around the world, standing with Christians facing persecution, strengthening them so that they may continue to share the gospel. Open Doors Canada is strengthening the body of Christ by providing Bibles and literature, preparing those who live in unstable environments to endure opposition, and equipping and mobilizing Christians in the free world to step up and help those whose freedoms have been stripped from them.

For more information about the persecuted Church, what we can do to help them, and what we can learn from them, contact your nearest office of Open Doors International. Here are the major English-speaking offices:

In Canada: https://opendoorscanada.org

In USA: https://opendoorsusa.org

In UK: https://opendoorsuk.org

In Australia: https://opendoors.org.au

In South Africa: https://opendoors.org.za

FOLLOW-UP DISCUSSION QUESTIONS FOR READERS AND SMALL GROUPS

1. Where is the red line for you in Jesus's teaching on turning the other cheek? If the damage is much worse than a slap on the cheek, is the response the same?

2. Where does self-defence fit into the biblical teaching on responding to opposition?

3. A theology professor said to me once, "They can hurt me all they want, but the minute they try to touch my wife and/or children, they will receive my full fury!" Does this statement resonate with you? If not, what is your response? Can we extend this support to the wives and children of other believers?

4. As a biblical follower of Jesus, how far do you go in defending freedom and opposing tyranny? What is the line you will not cross?

5. Which of the nine manifestos of John Dickerson resonates the most with you? Why?

6. Why is it so hard to balance grace and truth in your life? How do you expect to achieve it?

7. Which is harder for you: not to fear, hate, or harm?

8. Which of the three in question seven stated in the positive is most difficult?

9. Which biblical character outlined in this volume resonates the most with you? How?

10. What steps do you see yourself needing to take in your situation to become an overcomer like Aunty Mabel?

RECOMMENDED READING

CONTEMPORARY CHURCH AND SOCIETY

Dickerson, John S. *Hope of Nations: Standing Strong in A Post-Truth, Post Christian World.* Grand Rapids: Zondervan, 2018.

Dreher, Rod. *The Benedict Option: A Strategy for Christians in a Post-Christian Nation.* New York: Sentinel Books, 2017.

Dreher, Rod. *Live Not by Lies: A Manual For Christian Dissidents.* New York: Sentinel Books, 2020.

Eberstadt, Mary. *It's Dangerous to Believe: Religious Freedom and Its Enemies.* New York: Harper Collins Publishers, 2016.

Estabrooks, Paul and Cunningham, Jim. *Standing Strong Through the Storm: Victorious living for Christians facing pressure and persecution.* Third Edition. Milton, Ontario, Canada: Open Doors Canada, 2020.

Guinness, Os. *Impossible People: Christian Courage and the Struggle for the Soul of Civilization.* Downers Grove: InterVarsity Press, 2016.

Horowitz, David. *Dark Agenda: The War to Destroy Christian America.* West Palm Beach: Humanix Books, 2018.

Jeremiah, David. *Is This the End? Signs of God's Providence in a Disturbing New World.* Nashville: Thomas Nelson, 2016.

Jeremiah, David. *Agents of Babylon: What the Prophesies of Daniel Tell Us about the End of Days.* Carol Stream: Tyndale Publishers, 2015.

Kinnaman, David & Matlock, Mark. *Faith For Exiles: 5 Ways for a New Generation to Follow Jesus in Digital Babylon.* Grand Rapids: Baker Books, 2019.

Lutzer, Erwin W. *The Church in Babylon: Heeding the Call to Be a Light in the Darkness.* Chicago: Moody Press, 2018.

Lutzer, Erwin W. *We Will Not be Silenced.* Eugene, Oregon: Harvest House Publishers, 2020.

Mohler Jr., R. Albert. *The Gathering Storm: Secularism, Culture, and the Church.* Nashville: Thomas Nelson, 2020.

Nyquist, J. Paul. *Prepare: Living Your Faith In An Increasingly Hostile Culture.* Chicago: Moody Publishers, 2015.

Platt, David. *Counterculture: A Compassionate Call to Counter Culture in a World of Poverty, Same-sex Marriage, Racism, Sex Slavery, Immigration, Abortion, Persecution, Orphans, and Pornography.* Carol Stream: Tyndale Publishers, 2015.

Stetzer, Ed. *Christians In The Age of Outrage: How to bring our best when the world is at its worst.* Carol Stream: Tyndale House Publishers, 2018.

Teter, John. *The Power of the 72: Ordinary Disciples In Extraordinary Evangelism.* Downers Grove: InterVarsity Press, 2017.

Zahnd, Brian. *Postcards From Babylon: The Church in American Exile.* Spello Press, 2019. A very insightful and thought-provoking expose' of our non-biblical culture of materialism and militarism.

THE PERSECUTED CHURCH

Berhane, Helen. *Song of the Nightingale: One Woman's True Story of Faith and Persecution in Eritrea.* Colorado Springs: Authentic Media, 2009.

Boyd-MacMillan, Ronald. *Faith That Endures: The Essential Guide To The Persecuted Church.* Grand Rapids: Revell, 2006.

Brobbel, Floyd A. *Trouble on the Way: Persecution in the Christian Life.* Bartlesville: Genesis Publishing Group, 2021. Available from Voice of the Martyrs Canada.

Brunson, Andrew. *God's Hostage: A True Story of Persecution, Imprisonment and Perseverance.* Grand Rapids: Baker Books, 2019.

Estabrooks, Paul. *Secrets To Spiritual Success.* Second Edition. London: Amazon, 2022.

Estabrooks, Paul. *Night of a Million Miracles: The Inside Story of Project Pearl.* Santa Ana: Open Doors International, 2008. Available from Open Doors Canada.

Penner, Glenn M. *In the Shadow of the Cross: A Biblical Theology of Persecution and Discipleship.* Bartlesville: Living Sacrifice Books, 2004. Also available from Voice of the Martyrs Canada.

Rostampour, Maryam and Amirizadeh, Marziyeh. *Captive In Iran.* Carol Stream: Tyndale Publishers, 2013.

Sempangi, F. Kefa. *A Distant Grief: The real story behind the martyrdom of Christians in Uganda.* Glendale: Regal Books, 1979.

Ton, Josef. *Suffering, Martyrdom, and Rewards in Heaven.* Wheaton: Romanian Missionary Society, 2007.

ENDNOTES

INTRODUCTION

1. Glen H. Stassen, *Living the Sermon on the Mount: A Practical Hope for Grace and Deliverance* (San Francisco: Jossey-Bass, 2006).

CHAPTER ONE

2. Genesis 10 in Hebrew contains a list of 70 clans (somehow the Septuagint Greek translation ended up with 72 names of clans) from the three sons of Noah from which all the nations of the earth descended. In Jesus' day and in Jewish thought, this number was a symbolic representation of the nations of the world.

3. John Teter, *The Power of the 72: Ordinary Disciples in Extraordinary Evangelism* (Downers Grove: InterVarsity Press, 2017), 61.

4. Martin Luther King Jr., *Strength to Love* (Philadelphia: Fortress Press, 1981), 14.

5. King Jr., *Strength to Love*, 17

6. Charles Simeon, *Horae Homileticae: Matthew*, vol. 11 (London: Holdsworth and Ball), 318.

CHAPTER TWO

7. He shared his story at the Wilberforce Weekend of the Colson Center in Washington DC in mid-May 2019.

8. Breakpoint Email, December 18, 2018.

9. Jordan B. Peterson, *12 Rules for Life: An Antidote to Chaos* (Random House Canada, 2018), flyleaf cover.

10. Ed Stetzer, *Christians in the Age of Outrage: How to Bring Our Best When the World Is at Its Worst* (Carol Stream: Tyndale House Publishers, 2018), 2

11. John S. Dickerson, *Hope of Nations* (Grand Rapids: Zondervan, 2018), 44.

12. Sheila Gunn Reid, "Update School Board Votes to Close Cornerstone Christian Academy But Parent's Have a Plan," Rebel News (June 23, 2017).

13. Judge Perry, "Final Merits Hearing," Employment Tribunal Case #1304602/2018 (Birmingham: July 18, 2019).

14. "Employment Tribunal Rules Against Christian Doctor," ed. Colin Hart, The Christian Institute (October 2, 2019).

15. Mary Eberstadt, *It's Dangerous to Believe* (New York: Harper Collins Publishers), 2016.

16. K.A. Ellis, "Are US Christians Really 'Persecuted'?" *Christianity Today* (September, 2016), 36.

17. J. Paul Nyquist, *Prepare: Living Your Faith in an Increasingly Hostile Culture* (Chicago: Moody Publishing, 2015), 10.

18. Rod Dreher, *The Benedict Option: A Strategy for Christians in a Post-Christian Nation* (New York: Penguin Random House, 2018), 3.

19. Dreher, *The Benedict Option*, 3.

20. David Jeremiah, *Living with Confidence in a Chaotic World* (Nashville: Thomas Nelson, 2014).

21. David Jeremiah, *Is This the End? Signs of God's Providence in a Disturbing New World*, study guide (San Diego: Turning Point, 2016), 34.

22. Michael Gerson, and Peter Wehner, "How Christians Can Flourish in a Same-Sex-Marriage World," *Christianity Today* (November 2, 2015).

23. Matt Baume, "After Drew Brees Controversy, Hate Group Denies It's Anti-Gay," *OUT Magazine* (September 9, 2019).

24. Michael Brown, "Why So Much Hatred Against Christians in America Today?" Ask Dr. Brown (November 7, 2017).

25. Francis Schaeffer, *How Should We Then Live: The Rise and Decline of Western Thought and Culture* (Grand Rapids: Fleming Revell 1979).

26. Charles Colson and Nancy Pearcey, *How Now Shall We Live?* (Carol Stream: Tyndale House Publishers, 1999).

27. Os Guinness, *Impossible People: Christian Courage and the Struggle for the Soul of Civilization* (Downers Grove: InterVarsity Press, 2016), 164 Kindle.

28. Guinness, *Impossible People*, back cover.

29. Joseph Callahan, "The American War on Christians," *Huffington Post* (May 5, 2015).

CHAPTER THREE

30. David Platt, *Radical: Taking Back Your Faith from the American Dream* (Colorado Springs: Multnomah Publishers, 2010).

31. Alistair Begg, "Wholehearted Obedience" Truth For Life (May 16, 2018).

32. Barry Black, "Surviving as a Lamb in a Wolf's World," ASI Convention (St. Louis), 3ABN Youtube (March 25, 2013).

33. Os Guinness, *Impossible People: Christian Courage and the Struggle for the Soul of Civilization* (Downers Grove: InterVarsity Press, 2016), 294 Kindle.

34. Marina Hofman, *Women in the Bible Small Group Bible Study* (Burlington: Castle Quay Books, 2021), 76.

35. Andrew Chang, *The National* (September 1, 2019).

36. Charles R. Swindoll, *The Grace Awakening* (Dallas: Word Publishing, 1990) 13.

37. Sharon Hodde Miller, "Why Niceness Weakens Our Witness," *Christianity Today* (August 9, 2019). Adapted from her book, *Nice: Why We Love to Be Liked and How God Calls Us to More* (Grand Rapids: Baker Publishing, 2019).

38. Randy Alcorn, *The Grace and Truth Paradox: Responding with Christ-Like Balance* (Colorado Springs: Multnomah Books, 2009).

CHAPTER FOUR

39. Darrell W. Johnson, *Discipleship on The Edge: An Expository Journey Through the Book of Revelation* (Vancouver: Regent College Publishing, 2004), 395–396.

40. Further expanded in Paul Estabrooks and Jim Cunningham, *Standing Strong Through the Storm*, 3rd ed. (Milton: Open Doors-Canada, 2020).

41. Estabrooks and Cunningham, *Standing Strong Through the Storm*, 336.

42. Nicole Jansezian, "Peterson, Ben Shapiro Say Israel Called to Be a Light to the Nations," *All Israel News* (October 7, 2022).

43. Dietrich Bonhoeffer, *The Cost of Discipleship* (New York: MacMillan Publishing Company, 1959), 99.

44. Song written and sung by Ray Boltz, "I Pledge Allegiance to the Lamb," Allegiance (Nashville: Pinebrook Recording Studio, 1994).

CHAPTER FIVE
45. F. Kefa Sempangi, *A Distant Grief* (Glendale: G/L Publications, 1979), 119–121.
46. F. Kefa Sempangi, *From the Dust* (Eugene Oregon: Wipf & Stock, 2008), 2.
47. Sempangi, *A Distant Grief*, 11.
48. Fr. Boulos George, "A Message to Those Who Kill Us," Coptic Dad and Mom (April 9, 2017).
49. Jayson Casper, "Forgiveness: Muslims Moved as Coptic Christians Do the Unimaginable," *Christianity Today* (April 20, 2017).

CHAPTER SIX
50. *The High Tide and the Turn: A.D. 1914 to 2001*, ed. Ted Byfield, Vol. 12 (Edmonton: The Society to Explore and Record Christian History, 2013), 150–153.
51. Walter Wink, *Jesus and Nonviolence: A Third Way* (Minneapolis: Fortress Press, 2003), 5–6.
52. *The High Tide and the Turn*, 153.
53. *The High Tide and the Turn*, 151.
54. *The Christians: Their First Two Thousand Years*, ed. Ted Byfield, Vol. 12 (Edmonton: The Society to Explore and Record Christian History, 2013), 163–165
55. Rod Dreher, *Live Not by Lies: A Manual for Christian Dissidents* (New York: Sentinel, 2020), 157–158.
56. Dreher, *Live Not by Lies*, 4–5.
57. Dreher, *Live Not by Lies*, 6.
58. Dreher, *Live Not by Lies*, 210–211.
59. Dreher, *Live Not by Lies*, 206.
60. Guinness, *Impossible People*, 294 Kindle.

CHAPTER SEVEN
61. James R. Edward, "The Bonhoeffer That History Overlooked," *Christianity Today* (June 18, 2019).
62. Carl Lawrence, *The Church in China: How It Survives and Prospers Under Communism* (Minneapolis: Bethany House Publishers, 1985).
63. "Rethink," INcontext International Editorial (February 19, 2016).
64. Gustav Kros, "Just A Minute: To Be Transformed Again and Again and Again," INcontext (September 19, 2016).
65. This story is taken from Richard Wurmbrand, *In God's Underground* (Bartlesville: Living Sacrifice Book Company, 2004).

CHAPTER EIGHT
66. Erwin W. Lutzer, *The Church in Babylon: Heeding the Call to Be a Light in the Darkness* (Chicago: Moody Publishers, 2018), 42–43.
67. Gad Saad, *The Parasitic Mind: How Infectious Ideas Are Killing Common Sense* (Washington: Regnery Publishing, 2020), 123–124.
68. Randy Alcorn, *Safely Home* (Wheaton: Tyndale House Publishers, 2001), 30–33.
69. John Stonestreet, "The Issues For 2019: Looking Ahead," Breakpoint Daily Email, Colson Center For Christian Worldview (January 1, 2019).

70. Grayson Gilbert, "A Sign of the Times: When Persecution Comes from Within the Church," *Patheos Evangelical* (July 9, 2020).
71. The Septuagint is the earliest Greek translation of the Hebrew Old Testament.
72. Landa Cope, "The Power of One," *YouTube* (February 20, 2013).
73. Yi Wang, "My Declaration of Faithful Disobedience," China Partnership (October 4, 2018).

CHAPTER NINE
74. Hector Tamez, personal interview (1995).
75. These principles were first documented in my earlier book, *Standing Strong Through the Storm* (Milton: Open Doors International, 2003).
76. Nik Ripken, *The Insanity of Obedience* (Nashville: B&H Publishing, 2014), 91.
77. Maryam Rostampour, and Marziyeh Amirizadeh, *Captive in Iran* (Wheaton: Tyndale Publishers, 2013), 46.
78. Rostampour and Amirizadeh, *Captive in Iran*, 288.
79. Helen Berhane, *Song of the Nightingale* (Colorado Springs: Authentic Media, 2009), 75.
80. Joe Klein, "Why Not Kill Dictators with Kindness?, *Time* (March 3, 2003).

CHAPTER TEN
81. Mark Albrecht, World Evangelism Fellowship Religious Liberty Conference, e-mail (October 17, 2001).
82. Nicole Jansezian, "Jordan Peterson, Ben Shapiro Say Israel Called to Be a Light to the Nations," *All Israel News* (October 7, 2022).
83. John Loeffler, "The Coming Persecution of Christians in the West," WVW Broadcast Network, DVD (November 9, 2020).
84. Charles Pope, "The Five Stages of Religious Persecution," Community In Mission Blog (September 1, 2014).
85. David Jeremiah, *Is This The End?: Signs of God's Providence in a Disturbing World* (Nashville: Thomas Nelson Publishers, 2016).
86. In 1996, Professor Gregory Stanton, President of Genocide Watch, proposed a significant model of an eight-stage process of genocide in his works: "The 8 Stages of Genocide," and "The Genocidal Process," presented as the first Woking Paper (GS 01) of the Yale Program in Genocide Studies in 1998. There are interesting similarities between the opposition elements and the downward spiral to genocide as well as what psychologist Dr. John Gottman has labelled as the four most likely predictors of divorce in his book, *Why Marriages Succeed or Fail and How You Can Make Yours Last* (London: Bloomsbury Publishing PLC, 1997).

CHAPTER TWELVE
87. John Stonestreet, "The Benedict Option," Break Point This Week Email, Colson Center For Christian Worldview (March 17, 2017).
88. Michael Gerson and Peter Wehner, "How Christians Can Flourish in a Same-Sex-Marriage World," *Christianity Today* (November 2, 2015).
89. Gabriel Salguero, "Why Settle for the 'Wilberforce Option' When We Have Dr. King?" *Christianity Today* (November 2, 2015).
90. J. Paul Nyquist, *Prepare: Living Your Faith in an Increasingly Hostile Culture* (Chicago: Moody Publishers, 2015).

91. Glenn M. Penner, *In the Shadow of the Cross: A Biblical Theology of Persecution and Discipleship* (Bartlesville: Living Sacrifice Books, 2004).

92. Nyquist, *Prepare*, 18.

93. Nyquist, *Prepare*, 68.

94. Nyquist, *Prepare*, 153.

95 David Kinnaman, and Mark Matlock, *Faith for Exiles: 5 Ways for a New Generation to Follow Jesus in Digital Babylon* (Grand Rapids: Baker Books, 2019), 23.

96. Mark Matlock, *Faith for Exiles*, 11.

97. Mark Matlock, *Faith for Exiles*, 208.

98. John S. Dickerson, *Hope of Nations: Standing Strong in a Post-Truth, Post-Christian World* (Grand Rapids: Zondervan, 2018), 189–192.

99. Dickerson, *Hope of Nations*, 201–202

CHAPTER THIRTEEN

100. Jack Lee, "Arise O' Sleeper: Why the Church in America Needs to Prepare for Persecution," *Patheos Evangelica* (October 20, 2019).

OTHER TITLES BY
CASTLE QUAY BOOKS

WWW.CASTLEQUAYBOOKS.COM